THE TIMES
WAR

THE TIMES

WAR

A HISTORY IN PHOTOGRAPHS

Duncan Anderson

First published in 2003 by
TIMES BOOKS
HarperCollins*Publishers*
77-85 Fulham Palace Road
Hammersmith, London W6 8JB

The HarperCollins website address is
www.harpercollins.com

The Times is a registered trade mark of Times Newspapers Limited, a
subsidiary of News International plc

Printed and bound in Italy by
Editoriale Johnson

British Library cataloguing in Publication Data.
A catalogue record for this book is available from the British Library.

ISBN 0 0071 6498 X

Editorial:
Philip Parker
Terry Moore

Design:
Colin Brown

Copy-editing and proof-reading:
Margaret Gilbey

Index:
Janet Smy

Contents

Introduction

In the century and a half since Roger Fenton set up his apparatus on a battlefield in the Crimea, every war has attracted cameramen. The very first – Fenton, Felice Beato, James Robertson – did not think of themselves primarily as war photographers. War was just one amongst many subjects on which they worked. But as early as the 1860s a subdivision was emerging within their ranks. Matthew Brady, Alexander Gardner and John Burke saw themselves as different from other photographers, in part because of their subject matter, in part because of the risks they ran in capturing it on film. The evolution of the war photographer paralleled that of the evolution of the war correspondent. William Howard Russell's articles in *The Times*, describing the ineptitude with which the Crimean expedition was surrounded, triggered the despatch of Fenton to Balaclava because, unlike a journalist, a photograph couldn't lie, or so mid-Victorians believed, at least at the very infancy of the medium.

For a generation the war photographer and the war correspondent were complementary but different, until technology – the new light-weight cameras and dry developing processes of the late 1880s – allowed them to merge into a single entity, the photo-journalist. By the turn of the last century they had evolved a distinctive culture. Some, like Richard Harding Davis, Luigi Barzini, Jack London, Frank Hurley, Edgar Snow and Robert Capa, achieved immortality. Most are less well known, though their photographs would be recognised immediately.

Far more than any other profession, war photographers risk their lives. Fenton survived more by good luck than good management, driven by a desire to secure an action shot. As technology improved, the photographer could get ever closer to the action, in the belief that it was here that the reality of war would finally be captured. Robert Capa's pithy 'If your shots are no good then you aren't close enough' sums up this attitude. Capa always did get close enough – and was killed, along with hundreds of others, from Ridgway Glover, hacked to death by the Sioux in the Little Bighorn Mountains in 1866, to the dozens who have died so far in the early twenty-first century's 'War Against Terror'. When soldiers are taking cover, the photo-journalist is taking pictures – even platoon commanders on the Western Front in the First World War had a greater chance of survival.

Photographers want their pictures to have an impact. Sometimes they succeed, like the Somali cameramen, whose pictures of the mutilated bodies of American soldiers being dragged through the streets of Mogadishu in October 1993, served to trigger a US withdrawal. But more often they do not. Far more significant than the immediate impact, is the long-term significance. Human beings have visual memories. The moving image – either on film or television – is ephemeral; the still image, repeatedly published, and looked at again and again, attains iconic status. Our collective memories of conflict these past 150 years owe much to our ability to link these images into something like a B-movie that runs constantly in our memory banks. This book explores the creation of these icons.

Many people have helped with this book. I would like to thank Andrew Orgill and the staff of the library of the Royal Military Academy, Sandhurst, the best military history library in the English-speaking world, and the staff of News International's archives. Thanks are also due to Terry Moore, who has spent months in picture archives living with images of unadulterated horror, and to the designer Colin Brown and the copy-editor Margaret Gilbey. The book was conceived by Philip Parker of HarperCollins. Without his constant encouragement it would not have come to publication. Finally I should like to thank my wife Christine Gerrard, who interrupted her studies of the eighteenth century, to act as my first critic. The responsibility for errors and omissions are, however, entirely my own.

AMERICAN CIVIL WAR
1860–65

FRANCO-AUSTRIAN WAR 1859

CRIMEAN WAR 1853–56

INDIAN MUTINY
1857–59

OPIUM WAR 1856–60

ANGLO-BURMESE WAR 1853

FRENCH INVASION OF VIETNAM
1858–62

MAORI WARS 1860–61

The War Correspondent
and the War Photographer

THE MEETING

Early in June 1855 a meeting took place between two men in the British lines in front of Sebastopol which was to be of enormous symbolic importance in the history of war reporting. The world's first war photographer, Roger Fenton, newly arrived from England, persuaded the world's first war correspondent, William Howard Russell, to pose for him. Russell, his by now full beard reaching down to his chest, his hair hanging over the back of his collar, sat in a camp chair, clasping his hands before him. Having come badly equipped for the campaign, he had begged and borrowed clothes from sympathetic officers. He wore a commissariat officer's cap, a rifleman's patrol jacket and a pair of cord breeches, which he had tucked into calf-high butcher's boots. Pictured left, with his eyes partly hidden in a shadow cast by the peak of his cap, Russell's expression is one of thoughtful contemplation, as though trying to make sense of all he had seen since the spring of 1854.

We have no idea how these men regarded each other. Russell made no mention of Fenton in his diaries, and Fenton made only the brief comment 'I have got W. H. Russell's likeness' in a letter to his sponsor, William Agnew. It was Russell's presence which had brought Fenton to the Crimea. From the late autumn of 1854 the journalist's despatches in *The Times*, exposing incompetence, mismanagement and corruption, had enraged the British public and contributed to the collapse of prime minister Lord Aberdeen's government. In vain the military authorities, from commander-in-chief Lord Raglan down, had complained that Russell's despatches were grotesque caricatures and over-simplifications. The problem was how to expose Russell's mendacity, because even his worst critic allowed that Russell's descriptive powers were of unusual acuity. There was simply no one who could write with the same force as *The Times*' correspondent. The solution was not to attempt to match Russell with the written word, but to respond with a new technology then only 15 years old — the photograph — because everyone knew that the camera could not lie. Thus it was that, in their first campaign, the war correspondent and the war photographer were on different sides. More than a generation was to pass before new technology allowed the correspondent and the photographer to merge into a single being – the photo-journalist.

BACK BY EASTER

The 34-year-old Russell had been working on and off for *The Times* for 12 years, when in February 1854 *The Times*'s editor John Thaddeus Delane offered him a chance to join the British expedition setting out to face down the Russians and force them to withdraw their troops from Russo–Turkish border provinces in the Balkans. Delane told Russell he would be travelling with the Guards, that he would probably not go further than Malta and that he would be back by Easter. But Delane was wrong. The crisis with Russia was ostensibly the result of a long-standing dispute over Russian claims to the guardianship of the holy places in Palestine, then a province of the Turkish empire. In October 1853, when Russian troops entered the border provinces of Moldavia and Wallachia, which formed a neutralised buffer between the Russian and Turkish empires, Turkey declared war. Six weeks later a Russian fleet had sallied forth from its naval base at Sebastopol on the Crimean peninsula and attacked and sunk the Turkish fleet at its base at Sinope, near Constantinople. Britain and France both had reasons for supporting Turkey: Britain to protect her line of communications with India, and France, now led by Napoleon III, grandnephew of the great Napoleon, anxious to avenge the defeat of 1812 and establish legitimacy for the new Bonapartist dynasty. Less than a month after Russell received Delane's request, Britain and France were at war with Russia.

CROAKERS

Russell quickly discovered that Delane had been over-optimistic in expecting the military to co-operate. *The Times*'s correspondent was not, after all, permitted to travel with the Guards (there was no space for him on the transports) but was forced to make his own way overland, joining up with the convoy at Malta. The British commander-in-chief, Lord Raglan, had served as Wellington's military secretary in the peninsula, and had lost an arm at Waterloo. Now 66 years old, and commanding an army in the field for the first time in his life, Raglan decided to treat Russell just as Wellington had treated observers at the front reporting back to the newspapers some 40 years earlier. Officers in Wellington's army had written to the newspapers on a regular basis, frequently complaining about the conduct of the campaign. Wellington had called them 'croakers', had ostracised them and then used political allies in London to marginalise and neutralise them. This media policy had served the duke well, and Raglan would do the same. He could not stop Russell coming, but he planned to ignore him. It was not that Raglan wished to be personally rude to Russell – he was, in fact, an extremely polite and courteous man – it was simply that he had no conception of the latent power of Russell's pen.

The expedition to the East was the largest force Britain had so far despatched in such a short space of time, dwarfing those sent to America in 1776 and 1812, or to the Iberian peninsula in 1808 and 1809. British administrative arrangements, perfectly adequate for the despatch of regiments and brigades to South Africa and India, quickly broke down when required to deal with divisions and corps. The French, who were used to operating at divisional level and larger, and had had recent experience of sending substantial forces across the Mediterranean to fight in Algeria, coped far better. To Russell, whose knowledge of military

affairs was confined to reporting a brief skirmish between the Prussians and the Danes in 1850, the contrast was all too apparent. Reporting on the landing at Gallipoli on 8 April 1854, Russell was impressed by the ceaseless activity of the French: '. . . the daily arrival of their steamers and the admirable completeness of all their arrangements in every detail – hospitals for the sick, bread and biscuit bakeries, wagon trains for carrying stores and baggage – every necessary and comfort, indeed, at hand, the moment their ships came in'. By contrast, the British

... suffered exceedingly from cold. Some of them, officers as well as privates, had no beds to lie upon. None of the soldiers had more than their single regulation blanket. They therefore reversed the order of things and dressed to go to bed, putting on all their spare clothing before they tried to sleep. The worst thing was the continued want of comforts for the sick. Many of the men labouring under diseases contracted at Malta were obliged to stay in camp in the cold, with only one blanket under them, as there was no provision for them at the temporary hospital.

After several weeks based in Turkey, followed by deployment to Varna in Bulgaria, the expedition landed at Calamita Bay on the west coast of the Crimea, its objective to capture the Russian naval base at Sebastopol. Russell had already demonstrated a quite unusual ability to describe complicated events both vividly and with clarity, and was later to compare his eye to a lens and his pen to a camera. His description of the Anglo–French task force as it crossed the Black Sea evoked visions of a Turner seascape:

No pen could describe its effect upon the eye. Ere an hour had elapsed it had extended itself over half the circumference of the horizon. Possibly no expedition so complex and so terrible in its means of destruction, with such enormous power in engines of war and such capabilities of locomotion, was ever sent forth by any worldly power. The fleet, in five irregular and straggling lines, flanked by men-of-war and war steamers, advanced slowly, filling the atmosphere with

below
Fenton sits in a
wheelbarrow, in a study
to which he gave the
intentionally ironic title
'hardships of camp life'.
The viewer is reminded
that the army has now
been accommodated in
huts, a far cry from the
rigours of the first winter.
An officer wearing leather
overalls pours tea from a
Thermos flask, while the
remnants of a meal,
bread, cheese and a
bottle of wine, are clearly
visible in the foreground.
All in all, the life of a
soldier before Sebastopol
does not seem too bad.

below right
The area of operations
around Sebastopol,
showing the main
engagements. The map
shows the main tactical
problems. First, the right
(eastern) flank of the
Allies was virtually open,
so that the Russians
attacked on three
occasions – 25 October
and 5 November 1854,
and 16 August 1855.
Second, all Allied efforts
were confined to the
southern side of
Sebastopol Harbour,
allowing the Russians to
move in men and supplies
from the north.

innumerable columns of smoke, which gradually flattened out into streaks and joined the clouds, adding to the sombre appearance of the well named 'Black' Sea.

Russell's descriptive ability, his status as a barely tolerated outsider, and his lack of experience of British military operations, gave his despatches an extraordinary power. Compared with landings in the past, the disembarkation at Calamita Bay on 14 September proved unexceptional and was a good deal more efficient, for example, than the landing of Wellington's army at Mondego Bay in Portugal in 1809. But the inexperienced Russell, unaware that physical discomfort and being soaked to the skin are part and parcel of the soldier's condition, attributed all such episodes to military incompetence. He vigorously complained that

seldom or never were 27,000 Englishmen more miserable. No tents had been sent on shore, partly because there had been no time to land them, partly because there was no certainty of our being able to find carriage for them in case of a move. Towards night the sky looked very black and lowering; the wind rose, and the rain fell in torrents. The showers increased about midnight. And early in the morning fell in drenching sheets which pierced through the blankets and great-coats of the houseless and tentless soldiers.

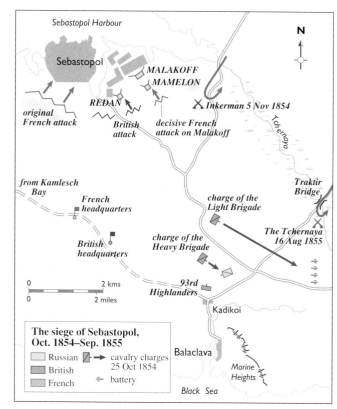

The siege of Sebastopol,
Oct. 1854–Sep. 1855

Russian		cavalry charges 25 Oct 1854
British		
French		battery

When they eventually saw Russell's accounts in *The Times*, the veterans of Salamanca and Waterloo dismissed him as yet another 'croaker'. But hard on the heels of the Calamita Bay account came Russell's description of the Battle of the Alma, when the British army, ably supported by the French, drove the Russians from a naturally strong defensive position. Years later Russell described his feelings as he tried to make sense of his first big battle: 'My eyes swam as I tried to make notes of what I had heard. I was worn out with excitement, fatigue and want of food.' His Alma despatch did the British army proud, and heroised the commander-in-chief. 'The men halted on the battlefield . . . and when Lord Raglan was in front of the Guards the whole army burst into a tremendous cheer, which made one's heart leap – the effect of that cheer can never be forgotten by those who heard it.'

'THE THIN RED LINE'

The Alma despatch established Russell's reputation for even-handed honesty. His criticism of incompetence was matched by unstinting praise for a good performance. A few weeks later, with the army established at Balaclava, the power of his pen was demonstrated with full force. On 25 October columns of a Russian relief army overran the positions of Britain's Turkish allies, and bore down on the harbour. For the moment the only force which opposed the charging Russian cavalry was the 93rd Highlanders, commanded by Sir Colin Campbell. Watching from a nearby hill, Russell described the Highlanders as 'that thin red streak tipped with a line of steel', a phrase which was soon to enter British popular consciousness as 'the thin red line'. He continued, '. . . With breathless suspense everyone awaited the bursting of the wave upon the line of Gaelic rock; but ere they came within two hundred and fifty yards, another deadly volley flashed from the levelled rifle and carried terror among the Russians. They wheeled about, opened files right and left and fled faster than they came.'

A short time later Russell witnessed the Charge of the Light Brigade. 'A more fearful spectacle was never witnessed than by those who, without the power to aid, beheld their heroic countrymen rushing to the arms of death. At a distance of 1,200 yards the whole line of the enemy belched forth, from thirty iron mouths, a flood of smoke and flame, through which hissed the deadly balls.' *Punch* magazine depicted a father reading Russell's despatch in *The Times*, waving a poker in the air with enthusiasm, while his sons jump with excitement and his wife and daughters weep. The despatch became the basis of the Poet Laureate Alfred, Lord Tennyson's *Charge of the Light Brigade*, the single most famous description of a military action in the English language. It remains to this day the best-known 20 minutes in British military history. Without Russell's pen it would have been yet another minor military disaster, its details known only to a handful of specialists.

The Balaclava despatch turned Russell into a household name. His fame was reinforced by his subsequent description of the Battle of Inkerman, the bloody hand-to-hand conflict fought to prevent a second Russian relief effort on 5 November. Now a national celebrity, with an avid readership, Russell's despatches detailing the collapse of the British administrative system in the autumn proved deadly. By this time he had many friends in the army and they were all talking. He could assert that 'generals who passed their youth in the Peninsular war, and had witnessed a good deal of fighting since that time in various parts of the world, were unanimous in declaring that they never knew or read of a war in which the officers were exposed to such hardships'. Forty years later in his reminiscences Russell said he 'could not tell lies to make things pleasant'. The tents were sometimes a foot deep in water and

. . . our men had neither warm nor waterproof clothing – they were out for twelve hours at a time in the trenches – they were plunged into the inevitable miseries of a winter campaign – and not a soul seemed to care for their comfort, or even for their lives. These were hard truths, which sooner or later must have come to the ears of the people of England. It was right they should know that the wretched beggar who wandered the streets of London in the rain led the life of a prince compared with the British soldiers who were fighting for their country, and who, we were complacently assured by the home authorities, were the best appointed army in Europe.

'THE CAMERA CANNOT LIE'

Russell's despatches did produce reforms to the commissariat and the medical services, but it was too little too late. A political storm broke in Britain, which on 1 February 1855 swept away the fragile Aberdeen coalition, and paved the way for the premiership of Lord Palmerston. Discussions between the Duke of Newcastle, the secretary of state for war, and Prince Albert, the Prince Consort, who took a deep interest in military affairs, gave rise to the idea of producing an irrefutable photographic record which would show that the army in the Crimea was now well looked after. The Prince, a firm patron of the Royal Photographic Society, was impressed by the way in which a sequence of photographs could be arranged to tell a story. He had first seen photography's narrative potential in a display of more than 1,500 pictures at the Great Exhibition some four years earlier. He already knew Roger Fenton, the honorary secretary of the society, who had taken portraits of the royal family the previous year. Fenton, the son of a Lancashire MP, had studied art in Paris under Paul Delaroche, who in 1839 had become fascinated by the possibilities of the daguerreotype. Influenced by Delaroche, by the early 1850s Fenton was one of Britain's leading society photographers, a mid-nineteenth-century Cecil Beaton. He could hardly resist the challenge of a photographic expedition to the Crimea, a patriotic mission which might also prove a

Fenton's assistant Marcus Sparling in the driving seat of the photographer's van, taken on 23 April, the day they took pictures under Russian fire in the 'Valley of Death'. This picture was Sparling's idea. Fenton wrote that his assistant 'suggested that as there was a possibility of a stop being put in the said valley to the further travels of both vehicle and driver, it would be a proper consideration for both to take a likeness of them before starting.'

major commercial success.

Thus it was that Fenton arrived in Balaclava on 9 March 1855. His first impression was that 'everything seems in much better order than *The Times* led me to expect'. He reported to his wife that 'Lord Raglan was in town this morning with his staff. The soldiers have nothing but good words to say about him; one of them told me that when the weather was at the worst he was constantly sitting about amongst the men'. But this favourable impression was soon undermined when he tried to get his equipment ashore. Fenton was accompanied by his servant William, a handyman and cook, and Marcus Spalding, a former corporal in the Light Dragoons, who was a gifted photographer himself and was to write a manual on the subject in 1856. The expedition came with 36 large cases crammed with equipment. They had five cameras of different sizes, about 700 glass plates contained in grooved wooden boxes, several chests of chemicals and a still for distilling water. In addition, they had a wine merchant's van, which they had converted into a mobile dark room. Fenton discovered that the harbour was controlled by different agencies, all with different chains of command. He met officer after officer who tried to be helpful, but didn't possess the necessary authority to secure a crane or a barge or docking space or labour. Eventually Fenton went to the captain of the *Mohawk*, a transport already at a dock, who transferred Fenton's carriage and supplies by boat to his own ship, from whence it was cross-decked on to a landing stage. Fenton wrote that this was a 'glorious example of the successful working of private enterprise'. He was sure 'it would have taken a week before by Government aid I could have disembarked my van'.

Before leaving Balaclava for the encampments, Fenton got Spalding to paint the self-explanatory slogan 'Photographic Van' on the side of the carriage, to avoid the persistent questions of curious onlookers. Ironically the slogan attracted rather than deterred attention. Soldiers flocked round the van, demanding that Fenton take their picture. He wrote to his wife, 'Everybody is bothering me for their portrait to send home; were I to listen to them and take the portrait of all comers I should be busy from now to Christmas and might make a regular gold digging in the Crimea.' At the end of March Fenton took the van out of Balaclava to the camps of the Guards and cavalry, where he took portraits, groups and views for several days. It was then dragged by stages up to headquarters.

Letters of introduction from Prince Albert to Lord Raglan and other commanders made Fenton (unlike Russell) *persona grata* with the military. Invited to dine with the commander-in-chief, he was placed on Lord Raglan's right, while the beautiful Lady George Paget, just arrived in the Crimea, was on Raglan's left, so that Fenton 'had plenty of conversation with her'. Fenton was entertained in a similar fashion by various subordinate commanders, and the French generals, and for several weeks was virtually attached to General Sir John Campbell's headquarters as one of his staff.

below
Fenton photographed in the uniform of a Zouave, the French colonial soldiers recruited in Algeria, who developed a formidable reputation in the Crimea. Fenton wrote admiringly about 'a dashing Zouave clad in a garb of many colours.'

Fenton's ambitions went well beyond panoramic and group shots. His correspondence was laced with attacks on the accuracy of conventional war artists from the *Illustrated London News* and other journals, whose sometimes fanciful depiction of events and scenes was the target of amused mockery from soldiers and officers. Satirical journalism also poked fun at the fashion for, but limitations of, the photographic medium. In 1854 *Punch* published a cartoon of a young lady writing to her fiancé in the Crimea. Gazing lovingly at his photograph she writes, 'I send you, dear Alfred, a complete photographic apparatus which will amuse you doubtlessly in your moments of leisure, and if you could send me home, dear, a good view of a nice battle, I should feel extremely obliged. P.S. If you could take the view, dear, just in the moment of victory, I should like it all the better.'

Although Fenton was constrained by the limitations of technology, he tried to transcend his medium by capturing action shots. After lunch on 15 April he set up his camera on Cathcart's Hill, one of the highest in the British lines, with his camera pointing towards the Garden fort, one of the Russian outposts to the south-west of Sebastopol. Thanks to his privileged position Fenton knew that the French had driven a mine

The Valley of Death, a
ravine behind the main
British artillery positions,
which became the
resting place for much of
the Russian counter-
battery fire which
overshot its targets.
Arguably the most
dangerous place in the
siege lines, Fenton knew
that Russian fire was at
its most fierce between
eight and ten in the
morning, and from three
to four in the afternoon.
He tried to reach the
valley at midday, but
was delayed until just
about 3 p.m. He spent
one and a half terrifying
hours in the valley and
survived entirely by
undeserved good luck.

under the fort, and were due to detonate it at 4 p.m. Fenton wrote, 'I was ready with my camera at the precise time, but no event coming off I shut up, and it was soon announced that it was postponed till half past six.' A few days later Fenton set up his apparatus in a ravine nicknamed the 'Valley of the Shadow of Death', which, lying behind British batteries, was filled with Russian cannon balls which had overshot their targets. As he prepared to take the picture, a Russian ball came over the lip of the ravine,

… bounding up towards us. It turned off when near, and where it went I did not see, as a shell came over about the same spot, knocked its fuse out and joined the mass of its brethren without bursting. It was plain that the line of fire was upon the very spot I had chosen, so very reluctantly I put up with another view of the valley 100 yards short of the best point. I brought the van down and fixed the camera and while levelling it another ball came in a more slanting direction, touching the rear of the batteries as the others, but instead of coming up the road, bounded onto the hill on our left about fifty yards from us and came down right to us, stopping at our feet. I picked it up and put it into the van; I hope to make you a present of it.

Fenton did his best, but was unable to get the shots he craved – the exploding mine or the bouncing cannon ball. He could have taken some sombre and haunting pictures of the aftermath of battle, but as a photographer 'embedded' into the British military system he felt morally unable to do so. On 2 June he rode along the route of the Light Brigade's charge seven months earlier and 'came upon many skeletons half buried, one was lying as if he had raised himself upon his elbow, the bare skull sticking up with just enough flesh left in the muscles to prevent it falling from the shoulders; another man's feet and hands were on the ground, the shoes on his feet, and the flesh gone'. Conscious of his mission, he also

left
The interior of the Barrack Battery, behind the Redan, taken by James
Robertson in September 1855. Robertson, chief engraver to the
imperial mint in Constantinople, was a gifted amateur photographer
who arrived in the Crimea with his Italian friend, the architectural
photographer Felice Beato at about the time Fenton left. William
Howard Russell recorded that guns of the Barrack battery had caused
heavy loss amongst the men of the Light Division on 10 September.

avoided taking pictures of anything which would suggest mismanagement, such as the organisation of
Balaclava harbour, about which he complained at great length in his letters.

Displayed at photograph exhibitions throughout Britain, and available as postcards and stereoscope
images, Fenton's collection was designed as an antidote to Russell's critical despatches. As his
correspondence shows, he often engaged in rigorous self-censorship. Popular expectations to the
contrary, the camera could, and did, lie.

THE DEVIL'S WIND

About the same time that Fenton photographed Russell, *The Times'* correspondent had another visitor, a
young, good-looking Indian gentleman named Azimullah Khan, a plenipotentiary for Nana Sahib, the
Rajah of Bitpur. Khan had decided to visit the Crimea on his way back to India from London, where he
had negotiated fruitlessly with the directors of the East India Company for the restoration of Nana Sahib's
pension, which had been cancelled on the death of his father in 1851. Russell, loquacious and fond of
brandy, talked at length with Khan about the nature of the British empire, and the systemic weaknesses
of the British army, so much in evidence in the Crimea. Khan, who had hitherto believed Britain an
invincible super-power, was soon regaling Nana Sahib in his palace at Cawnpore with these revelations.

There were other intimations of British weakness. On 26 November 1855 the British commander of
the city of Kars in eastern Anatolia, General Sir William Fenwick Williams, surrendered to besieging
Russians. Although the event is almost forgotten today, in late 1855 the British press regarded it as a
major disaster, because of the impact the fall of the city would have on British prestige in the East.
Editorials in *The Times*, the *Daily Telegraph* and the *Morning Post* predicted that Britain's failure to save
the city from the Russians would lead to disturbances in the more disaffected frontier regions of India.

In the spring and early summer of 1857 some sort of trouble was expected in India. It came not, as
expected, from the frontiers, but in the heart of Oudh, a province sprawling over the central plain of the
Ganges, which had been under British control since the beginning of the century. On 10 May soldiers of
the British East India Company's Bengal army based in Meerut, about 25 miles from Delhi, went on the
rampage, killing their British officers and any European civilians they could lay their hands on, including
women and children. What had gone wrong? For nearly a generation ship-loads of evangelical Christian
missionaries had been arriving in India, preaching against Islam and Hinduism, religions which they
dismissed as barbarous nonsense. At first the Indians ignored them, but soon evangelical policies were
being introduced by the company, not just the abolition of suttee, the burning of widows along with their
dead husbands, which many Hindus also opposed, but interference with the educational system, local
systems of inheritance, and the social position of women. The sense that a sustained attack on their
society was under way was reinforced in early 1857 by the introduction of the new Minie rifle, the
loading of which involved the soldier biting down on a greased cartridge; the Hindus believed the grease
to be the fat of the sacred cow, and the Moslems, the fat of the unclean pig. This violation of religious
scruples was too much for 85 cavalry sepoys at Meerut who, having refused to obey orders to bite the
cartridges, were tried by court martial and condemned to long prison sentences. It was the sight of these
soldiers being led away in chains, together with the growing apprehension that British power was based

on bluff, which led to the explosion of rage.

The following day mutineers crossed over the Jumna River on a bridge of boats and arrived in Delhi, where the garrison joined them in butchering all the Europeans they could find. The rebels declared as their new ruler the elderly Bahadur Shah, the hitherto powerless king of Delhi, last descendent of the Moguls, thereby transforming a military mutiny into a proto-nationalist uprising. Within the month the whole of the Ganges plain, from Delhi to the outskirts of Calcutta, was in rebel hands, with the exception of British garrisons which held out at Cawnpore and Lucknow, both deep in the heart of the most disaffected areas. At Cawnpore, Nana Sahib, who had been heavily influenced by Azimullah Khan, ordered his own small army to support the mutineers in besieging the residency, while he secured the surrender of the British with a promise of safe conduct downriver to Allahabad. On 27 June Nana's troops murdered the now disarmed men, and imprisoned the women and children, as they were embarking on river boats.

above
The bridge over the Gumti River, photographed by Felice Beato in the spring of 1858. It was this bridge which allowed British forces to advance to the final relief of Lucknow. William Howard Russell described it being built. 'The engineers are at work on the Gumti, throwing a floating bridge across. Already the men have cut down the bank and made a rough roadway to the water's edge, and the first raft of casks is in the steam.'

The first British counterattacks were now under way. In a series of astonishing forced marches, carried out at the height of the Indian summer in temperatures well over 100 degrees Fahrenheit, a column composed mainly of Highlanders under the command of Henry Havelock raced for Cawnpore, in what today would be called a hostage rescue mission. Smashing Nana's forces at Fatehpur on 12 July, and Anong on 15 July, the troops entered Cawnpore the following day to discover the bodies of British women and children prisoners hacked to death and thrown into a well by Nana's orders. Havelock, a fundamentalist Christian, and his now berserk Scots, swore vengeance on the heathen, and proceeded to hack their way through overwhelming rebel forces, fighting their way into Lucknow on 25 September, where they, too, were besieged. On 16 November, Sir Colin Campbell led a second relief force into the city, which allowed the survivors to be evacuated safely to Cawnpore. Meanwhile, another column under John Nicholson reached and stormed Delhi, killing thousands of mutineers and capturing Bahadur Shah. By now avenging British columns were cutting swathes along the Ganges, executing all Indians who might remotely be associated with the mutiny, which usually meant all able-bodied adult males. It was said it was possible to follow the march of the British by the bodies hanging from trees. The Indians now had a name for the avenging British – the Devil's Wind.

above

Executed Indians, taken by Felice Beato in the spring of 1858. Subsequent generations have seen this picture as an example of ruthless British repression, but at the time it was seen to epitomise British restraint. Beato could have taken pictures of trees festooned with corpses, and of Indians being flogged and humiliated before they were hanged. But he exercised remarkable self-censorship.

INTIMATIONS OF HORROR

Once again representing *The Times*, William Howard Russell landed at Calcutta on 18 January 1858, and immediately joined Sir Colin Campbell's army which was about to re-conquer the Ganges plain and extinguish the last embers of rebellion. This time Russell was thoroughly 'embedded'. He recorded Sir Colin saying to him, 'Now, Mr Russell, I'll be candid with you. We shall make a compact. You shall know everything that is going on. You shall see all my reports, and get every information that I have myself, on condition that you do not mention it in camp, or let it be known in any way, except in your letter to England.' About the same time, Felice Beato, a photographer of Italian birth who had filmed in the Crimea after Fenton had left, arrived in India with a commission from the War Office. Beato was primarily a photographer of architecture, who had worked around the Mediterranean, recording everything from the Borgias' palaces to Venetian fortresses. As areas were pacified the British wanted Beato to photograph the physical destruction of buildings, not just to maintain a record for its own sake, but to provide evidence of the effect of various types of shot against various types of masonry, an activity which is today called 'operational analysis'. Like Fenton in the Crimea, Beato had a mission, but this time the photographer and the journalist, though never in the same place at the same time, would work in tandem rather than in opposition.

above

Once one of the finest palaces in Lucknow, the Chutter Munzil had been fought over for more than eight months when Felice Beato took this picture in May 1858. Much of the structural damage had been caused by a mine exploded by the mutineers during the first siege, nearly a year earlier. The pock marks on the walls bear mute testimony to the intensity of the fighting.

At Cawnpore, Beato photographed the Bibighar, or 'House of the Ladies', the chambers where Nana Sahib had imprisoned the 206 women and children who had survived the massacre on the boats, before they too had been murdered. Beato chose an angle which cut out many of the Bibighar's windows and columns and, by concentrating on three small windows, a broken wall and a twisted tree, made the building look like a tomb. Even without knowing the history it is sinister, certainly not a place one would choose to spend the night. Russell also found it 'a horrible spot! Inside the shattered rooms, which had been the scene of such devoted suffering, are heaps of rubbish and filth. The entrenchment is used as a Cloaca Maxima by the natives, camp-followers, coolies, and others who bivouac in the sandy plains around it. The smells are revolting. Rows of gorged vultures sit with outspread wings on the mouldering parapets, or perch in clusters on the two or three leafless trees at the angle of the works by which we enter'.

On 16 March Campbell's army, now 30,000 strong, had reached Lucknow. Neither Russell nor Beato had expected such a large city, nor one with so many architecturally splendid buildings. Just days apart, both men climbed the same lofty minaret, so that they could describe the city in their different ways. Beato's photograph, skilfully composed, depicted Lucknow as a mid-Victorian eastern fantasy, a forest of marble domes, battlements and minarets. Russell, for once, felt overwhelmed by the scene. 'Alas, words! words! how poor you are to depict the scene which met the eye of the infidel from the quiet retreat of the muezzin! Lucknow, in its broad expanse of palaces, its groves and gardens, its courts and squares, its mosques and temples, its wide-spreading, squalid quarters of mean, close houses, amid which are kiosks and mansions of rich citizens, surrounded by trees, all lay at our feet, with the Dilkusha, and Martiniere, and distant Alumbagh plainly visible, and the umbrageous plains clothed in the richest vegetation, and covered with woodland, which encompasses the city. In the midst winds the Gumti, placid and silvery, though its waters are heavy with the dead.'

WAR PHOTOGRAPHY'S FIRST CONTROVERSY

Tasked with photographing the scenes of action, Beato made his way to the Secundra Bagh, a large palace on the eastern side of Lucknow which had been stormed by the Highlanders and Sikhs in November 1857. Here the British had taken heavy casualties, but had also killed more than 2,000

above

The Secundra Bagh, the focal point of mutineer resistance in the first battle for Lucknow, photographed by Felice Beato in March 1858. It was a massive, high-walled enclosure about 120 yards square, with carefully constructed narrow loopholes all around it, defended by about 3,000 Sepoys. Once British guns breached the walls, Highlanders and Sikhs stormed in, carrying out a fearful slaughter. Lieutenant Frederick Roberts, the future Field Marshal, wrote to his mother, 'I never saw such a sight. They were literally in heaps … You had to walk over them to cross the court.'

mutineers, whom they had buried in large pits. Beato's picture of the Secundra Bagh is his best known. The damage wrought by round-shot on the marble and masonry is clearly visible, and in the middle distance Beato has placed four Indians with a horse, to give a sense of scale.

The most controversial aspect of the picture are the dismembered skeletons which litter the foreground. This was the first time the dead had been shown after a battle, albeit one that had taken place four months earlier. When it was displayed in Britain the commander of the 93rd Highlanders, Colonel Maude, was surprised by the corpses, because 'every one was being regularly buried'. He presumed that 'the dogs had dug them up'. This led to the allegation that Beato had in fact arranged the bones in the manner of a still life to add to the composition. Another veteran of the battle, William Forbes Mitchell, flatly contradicted the colonel, writing that the British dead had been removed and buried in a deep trench, 'but the rebel dead had to be left to rot where they lay, a prey to the vulture by day and the jackal by night, for from the smallness of the relieving force no other course was possible'. It had taken just three years since Fenton set up his cameras in the Crimea for war photography to generate its first controversy.

opposite
Proclaiming 'Negro Sales' on a par with advertising the sale of china, glass and cigars, this sign on an Atlanta shop front was photographed by a northern cameraman in August 1864, after Sherman had captured the city. It was the sight of signs like this during his tour of the southern states in the spring of 1861, that pushed William Howard Russell firmly into the anti-slavery camp.

below
The young John Brown, who at a service in a congregational church at Hudson, Ohio in 1837 rose to his feet, raised his right hand, and said, 'Here before God, in the presence of these witnesses, I consecrate my life to the destruction of slavery.' On the morning of Brown's execution 22 years later Henry Wadsworth Longfellow wrote in his diary, 'This day will be a great day in our history, the date of the new Revolution – quite as much needed as the old one.'

The controversy would have been greater still if, like Russell, Beato had recorded everything he had seen. *The Times*' correspondent described in graphic detail the looting of the Kaiserbagh, a rambling palace which lay at the centre of the city. Beato photographed the exterior, but not the shambles which lay within. Similarly, Russell wrote movingly of the bodies of executed Indians which festooned trees all along the Ganges, many of whom, he suspected, were innocent men who happened to be in the wrong place when the 'Devil's Wind' swept by. British officers, many of whom were accomplished sketch artists, drew pictures of trees with bodies hanging like over-ripe fruit. Beato, mindful of his mission, exercised considerable self-censorship, confining himself to a single photograph of just two Indians swinging from a gibbet (see photograph, p. 21), which suggested that the British had exercised commendable self-control.

When Russell left for Britain in March 1859, British columns had smashed the mutineers' main armies, and the conflict had entered a long 'mopping-up' phase. The British pursued Nana Sahib into the jungles of Nepal, when the trail went cold, though for the next 30 years young British officers continued to arrest suspects. British agents traced Azimullah Khan to Calcutta, where he went to ground, emerging some time later in Constantinople. The Osama bin Ladens and Saddam Husseins of their day, Nana Sahib and Azimullah Khan became the embodiment of all that the British found dark in the Indian soul.

BULL RUN RUSSELL

On 16 October 1859, as the British continued their counter-insurgency campaign in India, a group of terrorists seized the United States' main arsenal at Harpers Ferry in Virginia, and captured local citizens as hostages. It was a classic example of what a hundred years later the Cuban revolutionary Che Guevara would call the 'Foco Theory', the idea that a dramatic action by a small group of determined men could plunge a society into crisis, and set in motion forces which would produce revolutionary change. The terrorists, only 19 in number, were led by John Brown, a fundamentalist Christian who believed that God had commanded him to bring an end to slavery in the United States through an apocalyptic uprising. Having succeeded in the first part of his operation, Brown issued a proclamation calling on the slaves of the south to desert their masters and come to Harpers Ferry, where they would be issued with arms. Few came, and a detachment of US Marines led by US Army Colonel Robert E. Lee soon captured Brown. He and six of his men were tried, convicted of treason and sent to the scaffold on 2 December. As far as the southern states were concerned the crisis was over, but it wasn't. The largest crowds ever seen in New York, Boston and Philadelphia gathered to register their protest against Brown's execution, for the great majority of the population in the north felt that Brown had been morally justified in what he had done and that his execution was judicial murder. The political knots which had kept the union together now unravelled at terrifying speed, leading to the election of Republican Abraham Lincoln to the

below

The American Civil War. Although a complex struggle, there were basically four areas of operations. First, a steady tightening of the US Navy's control over southern ports and the southern coast; second, an exhausting attritional struggle in northern Virginia; third, a campaign in the Mississippi valley culminating in the Federal capture of Vicksburg; and fourth, Sherman's 'march to the sea' and subsequent rampage through South and North Carolina. In essence the South was isolated, worn down, and then chopped into segments.

Presidency on 6 November 1860, and to the secession of South Carolina on 20 December.

Russell arrived in New York in March 1861, by which time another ten states had seceded, though it was by no means certain that war was inevitable. Introduced to the president in the still-unfinished White House, Russell recorded that 'Mr Lincoln put out his hand in a very friendly manner, and said, "Mr Russell, I am very glad to make your acquaintance, and to see you in this country. The London Times is one of the greatest powers in the world – in fact, I don't know of any thing which has much more power – except perhaps the Mississippi. I am glad to know you as its minister."' The meeting had left Russell 'agreeably impressed with his shrewdness, humour and natural sagacity'.

Months before the meeting, Russell had been impressed with a photograph of presidential candidate

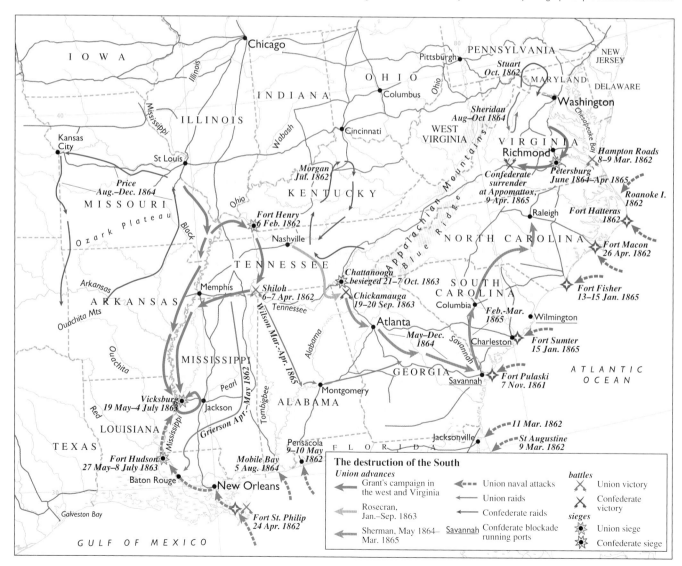

Manassas Junction, only 25 miles south-west of Washington, where the Manassas Gap Railway running 50 miles to the east from Winchester in the lower Shenandoah valley met the north–south line running from Washington to Charlottesville in central Virginia. On 21 July 1861 Confederate General Joseph E. Johnston used the line to rush reinforcements from Winchester to Manassas Junction, a move which allowed the Confederates to overwhelm the Union army as it advanced from the Bull Run. The high-speed locomotive ride down the Manassas Gap Railway (some engines reached nearly 50 miles per hour) was the first time trains had been used for the tactical movement of troops during a battle.

Lincoln, taken on 27 February 1860 in the Broadway studios of New York society photographer Matthew Brady. By constantly adjusting Lincoln's position, Brady had transformed the shambling unkempt backwoods lawyer, the first impression Lincoln often created, into a noble sage, whose eyes betokened humanity and wisdom, and it was this Lincoln that Russell met. On leaving the studio, Lincoln had gone to the Cooper Institute where he delivered a speech which established him as front runner for the presidency. Woodcut reproductions of Brady's portrait of Lincoln appeared in mass-circulation newspapers, while tens of thousands of photograph cards – known as *cartes de visite* – were printed and sold for about 25 cents each. Some time later, when asked if he knew Matthew Brady, Lincoln said that Brady and the Cooper Institute had made him president.

On the morning of 21 July 1861 correspondent and photographer were at last in the same spot at the same time, more or less. The war had begun three months earlier, when South Carolina had bombarded Fort Sumter, a federal fortification controlling Charleston harbour. Soon two volunteer armies had formed, one for the Confederacy to protect Richmond, the South's new capital, and one for the Union, to protect Washington. That morning the North's army set out for Manassas railway junction, where the

Confederate Army had positioned itself along Bull Run, a small tributary of the Potomac River. Loading his apparatus into a carriage, Brady had left Washington before dawn. He set up his camera on a hill near the small town of Centreville, which afforded excellent views of Manassas, about six miles distant. Here he was soon joined by the cream of Washington society, congressmen, senators, senior public officials and their wives. At first there were hundreds and then thousands, many equipped with picnic hampers and all set to enjoy the spectacle of the largest battle yet fought on American soil.

Russell had also tried to leave before dawn, but had been delayed by the American's reluctance to issue him with a pass. At about noon he reached Centreville. Russell reported that 'on a hill beside me there was a crowd of civilians on horseback, and in all sorts of vehicles, with a few of the fairer, if not gentler sex'. By now the battle was well under way: 'Clouds of smoke shifted and moved through the forest; and through the wavering mists of light blue smoke, and the thicker masses which rose commingling from the feet of men and the mouths of cannon, I could see the gleam of arms and the twinkling of bayonets.' Moving south to get a better view, Russell ran into a mass of wagons and men, all racing north. At first he thought they were returning to get more ammunition, but soon there was a mob: 'Emerging from the crowd a breathless man in the uniform of an officer with an empty scabbard dangling by his side was cut off by getting between my horse and a cart for a moment. "What is the matter, sir? What is all this about?" "Why, it means we are pretty badly whipped, that's the truth," he gasped.'

Russell was borne along on a human tide which carried all before it. 'The scene on the road had now assumed an aspect which has not a parallel in any description I have ever read. Infantry soldiers on mules and draught horses, with the harness clinging to their heels, as much frightened as their riders; negro servants on their masters' charges; ambulances crowded with unwounded soldiers; wagons swarming with men who threw out the contents in the road to make room, grinding through a shouting, screaming mass of men on foot, who were literally yelling with rage at every halt, and shrieking out, "Here are the cavalry! Will you get on?"' This portion of the force was evidently in discord.

As the mob swept past Centreville, it was reinforced by terrified senators and congressmen, whose carriages became part of the utter rout. Brady's carriage was overturned and Brady himself was found wandering in a confused state by some officers of a New York regiment who recognised him and gave him a sword. He made it safely back to Washington – he was never quite sure how – and the following day had his picture taken in what was then recognised as the photographer's dress uniform – long white dust jacket and broad-brimmed straw hat. He inscribed the picture 'Brady, The Photographer, returned from Bull Run. Photo taken July 22 1861' and used it as a publicity shot throughout the war. Russell sent his description of the Bull Run rout to *The Times* and then concentrated on other stories, as Northern panic subsided.

Four weeks later, when *The Times* 'Bull Run' edition arrived in New York, a storm broke over Russell. Americans had, of course, said exactly the same things, but in the interval rationalisations had been invented. Russell's story tore open a freshly healed wound. It would have been bad enough if an American had done this, but Russell was British. One by one his sources of information closed down, until he was left with no choice but to return to London.

right

Matthew Brady, photographed the day after he had returned from the debacle at Bull Run. The outline of the sword he was given by officers from a New York regiment, who found him wandering near Centerville, can be seen under the left hand side of his dust jacket. His attempts to maintain an army of photographers in the field led to his financial ruin. He descended into depression and alcoholism and died in the paupers' ward of a New York hospital in 1896.

Photo taken
July 22nd
1861

graphe

Run

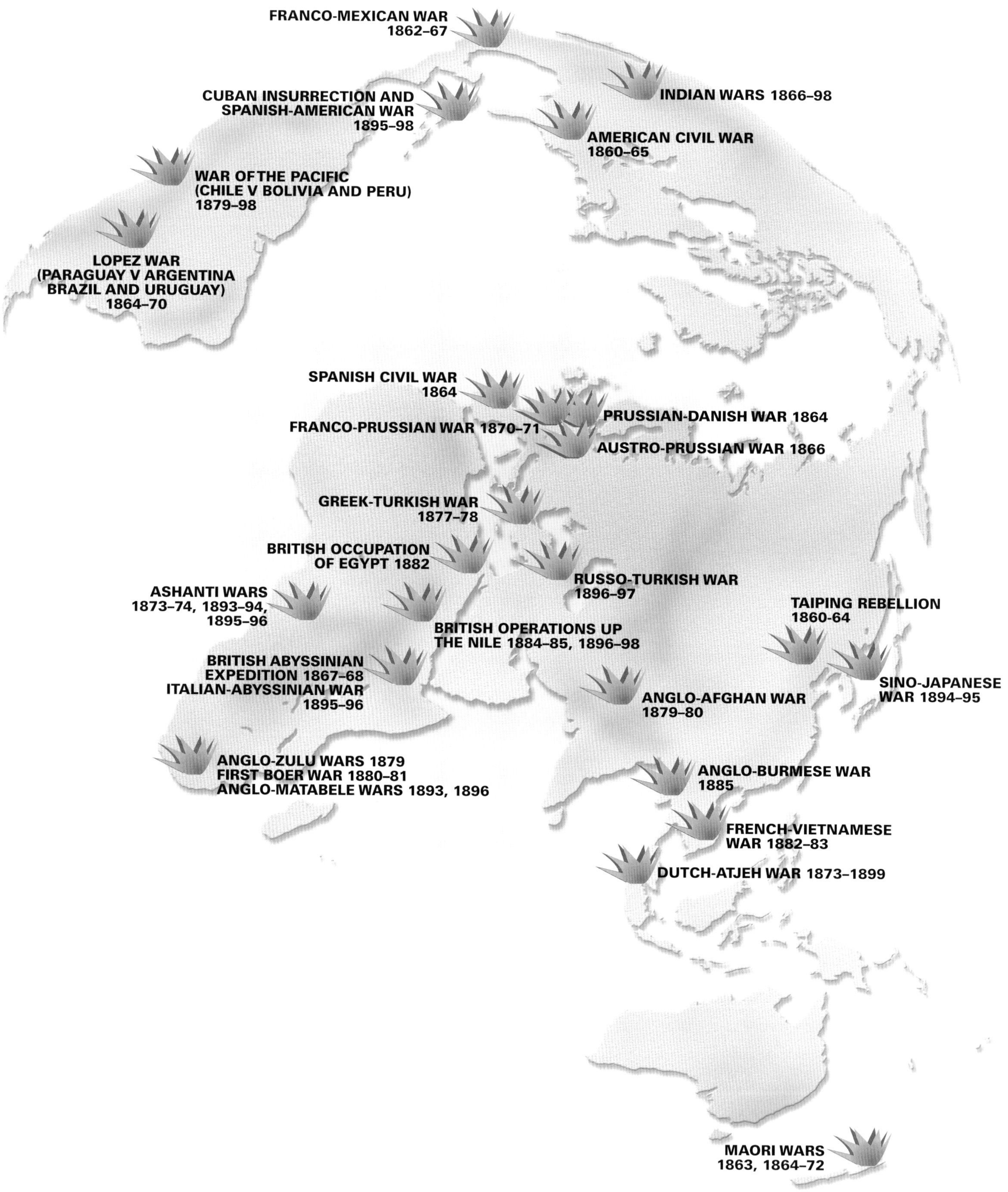

FRANCO-MEXICAN WAR
1862–67

INDIAN WARS 1866–98

CUBAN INSURRECTION AND
SPANISH-AMERICAN WAR
1895–98

AMERICAN CIVIL WAR
1860–65

WAR OF THE PACIFIC
(CHILE V BOLIVIA AND PERU)
1879–98

LOPEZ WAR
(PARAGUAY V ARGENTINA
BRAZIL AND URUGUAY)
1864–70

SPANISH CIVIL WAR
1864

PRUSSIAN-DANISH WAR 1864

FRANCO-PRUSSIAN WAR 1870–71

AUSTRO-PRUSSIAN WAR 1866

GREEK-TURKISH WAR
1877–78

BRITISH OCCUPATION
OF EGYPT 1882

RUSSO-TURKISH WAR
1896–97

ASHANTI WARS
1873–74, 1893–94,
1895–96

TAIPING REBELLION
1860-64

BRITISH OPERATIONS UP
THE NILE 1884–85, 1896–98

BRITISH ABYSSINIAN
EXPEDITION 1867–68
ITALIAN-ABYSSINIAN WAR
1895–96

SINO-JAPANESE
WAR 1894–95

ANGLO-AFGHAN WAR
1879–80

ANGLO-ZULU WARS 1879
FIRST BOER WAR 1880–81
ANGLO-MATABELE WARS 1893, 1896

ANGLO-BURMESE WAR
1885

FRENCH-VIETNAMESE
WAR 1882–83

DUTCH-ATJEH WAR 1873–1899

MAORI WARS
1863, 1864–72

Photographing Total War

THE AMERICAN EXPERIENCE, 1861–65

Even before Bull Run, Russell, who had toured the Confederacy, had confided to his diary that the Union 'will not have it over the South without a tremendous and long-sustained contest, in which they must put forth every exertion, and use all the resources and superior means they so abundantly possess'. The defeat at Manassas Junction convinced the North that it had to mobilise on the same scale as the infant French republic in 1792, and prepare to wage a war which would last years rather than months, and which might come to involve potentially hostile European powers like Britain and France. By contrast the Confederacy relaxed, being convinced by Manassas of its innate military superiority, and certain that Britain and France would have to intervene to secure supplies of cotton for the mills of Manchester and Lyon.

To American photographers it was clear that the war would create a demand for images. Before Bull Run the pictures of one of Brady's former employees, George S. Cook, were on sale in New York. Cook, a southerner, had returned to New Orleans during the secession crisis, and had then travelled up to Charleston. At the beginning of April 1861, Cook had talked his way into Fort Sumter to photograph Major Robert Anderson, who had refused to surrender his garrison to the Confederacy. A few weeks later Anderson's card photograph was selling like hot cakes in New York, at 50 cents a copy, twice what Brady had got for Lincoln's photograph a year earlier. On 13 April, the day Anderson surrendered, southern photographers swarmed over the fort, taking dramatic pictures of battle damage, similar to those taken by Beato in India.

right
The open top tier of Fort Sumter. At 04.30, 12 April 1861, 70 Confederate guns, firing in rotation, opened up on Fort Sumter. A witness recalled, '... a perfect sheet of flame flashed out, a deafening roar, a rumbling deadening sound, and the war was on.' During the next 34 hours Confederate batteries fired 4,000 shells, which Sumter's 85 soldiers and 43 workmen found impossible to match from their own cannon. Their commander, Major Robert Anderson, surrendered early in the afternoon of 13 April, and marched his garrison out under their colours the next morning.

After this first splurge, however, Southern photographers quickly ran short of photographic materials, none of which were produced in the Confederacy. Moreover, unlike the cities of the North, which were utterly remote from the war, there was little demand for battle scenes in the South, where the reality of war came closer month by month. Southern photographers rationed their increasingly scarce stocks for the photograph which was always in demand, the portrait of the husband, father or son in the uniform of the Confederacy, taken before he left for war.

In the North, Brady had originally planned to produce a single volume of photographs, rather like Fenton's collection from the Crimea. As the conflict became increasingly total, Brady realised he would have to organise his photography on the same basis as other aspects of the North's war effort – its scale would have to be industrial. Brady began by hiring about 20 skilled photographers, assigned them to various units and spent about 100,000 dollars paying for all their supplies and equipment. He took relatively few pictures himself, but was rather like the chairman of a photography industry, who was part entrepreneur, part director of photography, but also part artist. More than 300 photographers took pictures of various aspects of the American Civil War, about half of whom worked for Brady at one time or another.

BREAKING THE TABOO

One of Brady's assistants, Alexander Gardner, a Scot who had emigrated to America in 1849, pushed the limits of what was thought acceptable in September 1862, by photographing the corpses of Confederate soldiers killed at Antietam. When the collection was displayed in New York about three weeks later it caused a sensation. An editorial in the *New York Times* thought that 'Mr Brady has done something to bring home to us the terrible reality and earnestness of war. If he has not brought bodies and laid them on our dooryard and along the streets, he has done something very like it … It seems somewhat singular that the same sun that looked down on the faces of the slain, blistering them, blotting out from the bodies all the semblance to humanity, and hastening corruption, should have thus caught their features upon canvas, and given them perpetuity for ever. But it is so'.

Propelled by an apparently insatiable demand for photographs, Brady's empire expanded very rapidly, and then, like all such enterprises, began to fragment. Having already, thanks to Antietam, established a reputation as a daring and innovative photographer, Gardner broke away in

above

'The Harvest of Death.' Hoping to inflict a crushing defeat on the Union, in June 1863 Lee invaded the North, colliding with a Union army under Meade at the Pennsylvanian town of Gettysburg on 1 July. After two days of probing attacks, on 3 July Lee launched four divisions, one of which was commanded by Major General George E. Pickett, at the centre of the Union line. The result was a slaughter, known conveniently but inaccurately as Pickett's Charge. Sullivan visited the site two days later, when the sweltering heat of the July sun had already caused the decomposing bodies to bloat.

1862, and others soon followed. Competition between Brady's and Gardner's enterprises was intense. On 5 July 1863, Timothy H. O'Sullivan, a former Brady employee who had defected to Gardner, took the most famous photograph of the war, *The Harvest of Death*, an arrangement of enemy dead on the Gettysburg battlefield. Brady hurried to the battlefield but arrived too late. The Gardner team had ensured that, by the time Brady got there, all the best bodies had been buried.

Brady, Gardner and their teams were concerned not just with portraying the aftermath of battle, but with recording the process by which a society geared itself up for total war. They took pictures of American munitions factories working at full blast, of railroads moving ammunition and cannon, and of vast military encampments, where thousands of men drilled in serried ranks. They also catalogued a new type of war, though at the time they didn't realise what they were doing. Fenton and his successors had photographed the siege lines around Sebastopol, and American cameramen took pictures of trenches at Petersburg. In so doing they captured on film one of the consequences of industrial war. The trench systems in Northern Virginia in 1864 and 1865 were not concentrated around a single defended locality, but snaked for 10 and then 20, and then finally for nearly 30 miles, before the Confederacy ran

top

As Sherman's troops moved out of Atlanta on 15 November 1864, stay-behind parties created a swathe of destruction in the city. Photographer George N. Barnard captured the manufacture of 'Sherman's neckties', iron rails heated on burning sleepers until hot, and then twisted into a circle.

out of soldiers to put in them.

Photographers also detailed the pulverising of the South. Seventy-eight years before Spaatz's and Eaker's B-17 bombers cut a swathe of destruction across Hitler's Third Reich, Sherman's cavalry columns had wreaked havoc throughout Jefferson Davis's Confederacy. Like the B-17 crews, who had to photograph the results of each mission, Sherman's cavalry was accompanied by photographers. One of the best known, the 23-year-old George N. Barnard, catalogued the results of Sherman's 'March to the Sea', the burning of Atlanta, the systematic destruction of the railway and telegraph system, and the razing of Columbia, Charleston, Richmond and many other Southern cities and towns.

Competing ruthlessly against each other, photographers strove to overcome the limitations of technology to produce the still-elusive action shot. On 8 September 1863 George S. Cook set up his camera on the ruins of Fort Sumter to photograph US monitors bombarding Fort Moultrie. Cook, in the direct line of fire, caught the warships at the moment of opening fire. One of the balls narrowly missed him, while another knocked one of his plate holders off the parapet into a rainwater cistern. During the Battle of Seven Pines, another of Brady's assistants managed to persuade Union gunners to stand still while they were actually repelling attacks by 'Stonewall' Jackson's soldiers, long enough for him to get an exposure. In 1899 Captain A. J. Russell recalled watching photographer T. C. Roche take pictures during artillery duels in the trenches before Petersburg in the autumn of 1864:

above

Seized by 30,000 Federal troops commanded by General Butler on 5 May 1864, the Confederate arsenal at City Point on the southern bank of the James River in northern Virginia was destroyed by a vast explosion on 9 August, which killed and injured 169 people and reduced the buildings to burnt-out shells. Despite the structural damage, the docking area and rail system remained intact, which allowed the Federal army to continue to use City Point as its own depot for munitions and ordnance.

He had taken a number of views and had but one more to make to finish up the most interesting views, and this one was to be from the most exposed position. He was within a few rods of the place when down came with the whirlwind a ten-inch shell, which exploded, throwing the dirt in all directions; but nothing daunted and shaking the dirt from his head and camera, he quickly moved to the spot, and placing it over a pit made by the explosion, exposed his plate so coolly as if there were no danger, as if working in a country barnyard. The work finished, he quickly

folded his tripod and returned to cover. I asked him if he was scared. 'Scared?' he said. 'Two shots never fell in the same place.'

By early 1865 Gardner was trying to overcome the limitations imposed by the long exposure time needed, by setting up several cameras in the same location to photograph the same predictable events – parades, funerals, executions and so on – at intervals of a few seconds. When arranged in chronological sequence, the photographs would tell a story visually. Like all great innovators he had foreseen possibilities – in this case the cinema – about 30 years before various technical developments would make it possible.

The Civil War photographers produced images on a scale which had been unimaginable only ten years earlier. In 1851 visitors to London's Great Exhibition had been astonished by a display of more than 1,500 photographs, more visual images than ever before had been displayed at one time and in one place. These images had been the product of scores of photographers hard at work over the preceding decade. We have no idea of how many photographic images were produced in North America between 1861 and 1865, though some estimates put it as high as a quarter of a million. When Gardner left Brady, for example, he took with him some of his best negatives, and in September 1863 started his own mail order business, 'Photographic Incidents of the War', which offered a customer a selection of nearly 600 images. Today, libraries and museums have catalogued more than 18,000, of which 7,000 have been attributed to the Brady organisation.

It is not just the sheer size of the Civil War photographic legacy, but the quality of many of the

above

In April 1865 Gardner visited the site of the battle of Cold Harbor, only ten miles north-east of Richmond, where Grant had lost 7,000 men in one hour in fruitless frontal attacks on Lee's strongly fortified positions. The bodies of the Union dead had been lying in the open for ten months. In his sketchbook of the American Civil War Gardner wrote, 'It speaks ill of the residents of that part of Virginia, that they allowed even the remains of those they considered enemies to decay untended where they fell.'

below

Giuseppe Garibaldi, revered in Italy as the father of the modern nation, photographed about 1860). By this time Garibaldi had become the most famous international revolutionary of the nineteenth century. In the 1830s and 40s he had fought with insurgents in Brazil and Argentina, raising an Italian legion, identified by wearing red shirts. Garibaldi and his Red Shirts fought campaigns in Italy in 1848–49, 1859, 1862 and 1866 to drive out the Austrians and secure unification, and fought again on behalf of the French Third Republic against the Prussians in 1870. Garibaldi supported the formation of trade unions, the introduction of universal manhood suffrage, universal compulsory education, and supported the Union against the Confederacy, Denmark against Prussia, and Poland against Russia. Wherever a liberal, progressive, nationalist cause was under threat between the mid 1840s and 1870, there was a good chance that Garibaldi and his Red Shirts would turn up.

photographs, which continues to surprise and delight historians. Under the pressure of a war for national survival, and locked in a no-less-deadly struggle with their competitors, many of the photographers were able to produce images which were not to be equalled until the 1890s, when technological advances made photography increasingly foolproof.

PHOTOGRAPHING LIMITED WAR – THE EUROPEAN EXPERIENCE, 1859–78

Between 1859 and 1878 Europe witnessed eight major conflicts. Two of these, the Franco–Austrian War (June–Oct 1859) and Garibaldi's invasion of Sicily and the Kingdom of Naples (1860–62), were part of the process by which Italy was to be unified. There were another three conflicts which involved the fragmentation of states and empires: Poland rose in bloody insurrection against Russia between 1863 and 1864; between 1874 and 1875 Spain lapsed back into civil war for the third time in the nineteenth century; and disturbances within the Christian Balkan provinces of the Turkish empire led to conflict with Russia (1877–78), and almost to a general European war. There were three further conflicts, a war between a German–Austrian coalition and Denmark over the border provinces of Schleswig-Holstein (1864), a war between Prussia and Austria to decide who was going to be the leader of the Germanic world (1866) and a war between France and Prussia (1870–71) to determine which nation would be dominant in Europe. The last three conflicts were the classic 'Kabinet Kriegs' by which Prussian Chancellor Count Otto von Bismarck sought to effect the unification of Germany. Described as 'Froehliche Kleine Kriege' ('Jolly Little Wars'), there was nevertheless a danger that they could have developed into something very much larger.

The first of these conflicts was over almost before the rest of Europe realised what was happening. On 23 April 1859, in conditions of the greatest secrecy, a French army under the personal command of Napoleon III moved into northern Italy to support the proto-Italian state of Sardinia–Savoy against the Austrian empire. In a whirlwind campaign the French achieved crushing victories at Magenta on 4 June and at Solferino 20 days later, after which Austria sued for peace. Eight weeks was simply not enough time to mobilise correspondents and photographers, even if the French and Austrians had been disposed to offer them freedom of movement, which they were not.

ITALIAN PIN-UPS

Unlike the army of the Second Empire, Garibaldi's insurgents needed publicity, and courted newspapers and photographers. But this was only possible when they were in exile, not trekking in Sicilian mountains, so that most photographs of this period depict handsome, dashingly bearded Italian guerrillas in heroic poses. Photographs of Garibaldi and the insurgent poet Mazzini decorated the bedroom walls of thousands of middle-class young women in London, Paris and Berlin, in much the same manner that posters

right

A triumphal photograph which backfired. Prussian photographs taken after the capture of the Danish fortress of Dybbol in April 1864 were intended to celebrate the success of Prussian arms, and pictures like this hung in the officers' messes of various Prussian regiments for the rest of the century. But they also served to remind the viewer that a relative handful of Danes had held up the Prussian advance for more than a month, in a classic David versus Goliath conflict. Prussia, which had very good claims on the territory of Schleswig-Holstein, emerged as an expansionist bully. The effect on British opinion was particularly marked, and was the first intimation that Anglo–Prussian friendship, a given over the preceding century, might not survive another bout of Bismarckian expansion.

of Che Guevara would hang on the walls of their granddaughters' bedrooms 100 years later. The Polish insurgents who rose up against the Russian empire in January 1863 also wanted publicity, but western correspondents were forbidden entry into Russian territory, and Britain and France had to make do with reports produced by Polish exile groups. Nor could the Poles hope for sympathy from within the Russian intelligentsia; Leo Tolstoy, for example, who had served in the siege of Sebastopol, advocated crushing the Poles with extreme ferocity, advice which the Russian army followed with enthusiasm. The last embers of the revolt had been extinguished by the early summer of 1864.

On 1 February 1864, while Anglo–French attention was focused on America and on the Polish revolt against Russia, a largely Prussian Army, with some Austrian assistance, crossed the Danish border and struck into the disputed provinces of Schleswig-Holstein. The Prussians expected a quick victory, but on 15 March the advance was held up at the Danish fortress of Dybbol, on the Baltic coast of Schleswig, which the Prussians were forced to besiege. With sea lanes open, the Danes were able to communicate their stand to the rest of the world, which immediately began to side with the gallant 'David' resisting the overwhelming power of Prussia's 'Goliath'. By April 40,000 Prussians were concentrated against the fort, subjecting it to an average of 500 artillery rounds per day. The garrison, only 5,000 strong, was steadily whittled down. By the time the Prussians made their final successful assault on 17 April, more than 1,800 of the defenders had been killed or wounded. Dybbol became a national symbol to the Danes, and even today a tour of the ruins is an essential part of the education of Danish school-children. Because the army had been static for more than a month, photographers had ample opportunities to photograph the operations, and to capture the picture that every officer's mess in Prussia wanted, that of their men standing on the main redoubt, beneath the Prussian flag flying triumphantly in the breeze.

At dawn on 16 June 1866 Prussian columns struck into the Austrian province of Bohemia, and 17 days later inflicted a crushing defeat on the Austrian Army at Koniggratz on the Elbe. William Howard

Russell had arrived in Vienna just before the outbreak of hostilities, and covered the war from the Austrian side, reporting on Koniggratz from the top of a church steeple. This was the biggest battle fought in Europe since Leipzig in 1813, with about a quarter of a million Prussians and some 215,000 Austrians and Saxons converging on an area of about 20 square miles. For once Russell felt overwhelmed by the task. He wrote: 'Nothing but a delicate and yet bold panorama on a gigantic scale could convey any idea of the scene, filled with over half a million of men, moving over its surface like the waves of the sea or as a vast driving cloud in a gale.' There were photographic teams chasing both the Prussian and Austrian armies, but added to the problems of lengthy exposure and smoke was the as yet insurmountable photographic obstacle of a battle fought in driving rain.

'SUCH HORRIBLE SHAPES'

In Bismarck's next war, the conflict with France he cleverly provoked in the summer of 1870, William Howard Russell was an honoured guest of the Prussian political and military hierarchy. Bismarck, who, like Lincoln, recognised the power of *The Times*, gave Russell detailed briefings in his excellent if accented English. After some initial confusion Russell went on campaign, embedded in the Crown Prince's headquarters. At the end of August the Prussian armies, numbering more than 200,000, had trapped the 121,000-strong main French army, commanded by Napoleon III in person, at Sedan. High on the ridges overlooking the city, the Prussians placed nearly 500 of their new Krupps-manufactured breech-loading iron guns, which had a greater range and a higher rate of fire than French artillery.

On the morning of 1 September the Prussian guns opened up a bombardment which was the heaviest and most intense so far experienced in the history of war. The French attempted to break out, first to the north and then to the south, but their formations were shredded by Prussian artillery fire. Standing on one of the ridges overlooking the city, Russell had a ring-side seat. He wrote that he 'could almost look into Sedan. I could see soldiers on the ramparts, citizens in the street . . . It is not a pleasant thing to be a mere spectator of such scenes. There is something cold-blooded in standing with a glass to your eye, seeing men blown to pieces, or dragging their shattered bodies to places of safety, or writhing on the ground too far from help, even if you could render it'. With his army in a hopeless position, that evening Napoleon III capitulated.

Two days later Russell walked over the battlefield. The casualties, 17,000 French and 9,000 Prussians, were not as heavy as the casualties at Antietam or Gettysburg, but Russell realised that they had died in new ways. He reminded his readers that he had had 'many years experience of the work of war', but that he had 'never seen the like before'. There were mounds of Prussian corpses, their bodies riddled with bullets, who had been mown down by the French Mitrailleuse, a terrifying hand-cranked machine-gun. But the real horror had been produced by the sheer intensity of Prussian artillery fire. He 'had never beheld death in such horrible shapes – because the dead had on their faces the expression of terror – mental and bodily agony such as I never should have thought it possible for mortal clay to retain after the spirit had fled through the hideous portals fashioned by the iron hand of artillery. There were human hands detached from the arms and hanging up in the trees; feet and legs lying far apart from the bodies to which they belonged'. Russell's despatch was a warning of the reality of industrial war, where a gallant

'thin red streak tipped with steel' would be obliterated within seconds.

THE SEDAN PHOTOGRAPH

There was at least one photographer at Sedan, and a single photograph survives, which purports to show
Prussian infantry attacking up a slope, supported by lines of infantry moving up in reserve. Unfortunately,
the photograph has been heavily retouched. The Prussians in the foreground are standing far too
nonchalantly for men who would have seen the effects of the Mitrailleuse. In addition, the men in the
far distance would have had to be about 20 feet tall in order to be picked up at that range by any camera
of the period, and were clearly a later addition, as were the puffs of white smoke which drift across the
picture, apparently independent of any artillery. Had the cameraman been of the quality of Gardner or
O'Sullivan, we might well have had a visual record of what Russell had seen, and it is less likely that
his warning about the way in which war was changing would have been so soon forgotten.

Bismarck thought the war would end with the capitulation of Napoleon III, but the people of France
thought otherwise. In Paris on 4 September a meeting of the National Assembly abolished the monarchy,
inaugurated a new Republic (the third) and began forming massive citizen armies. By 19 September Prussian
forces had encircled Paris, but the Prussian chief of staff, Helmut von Moltke, had no intention of playing
to French strengths, and he therefore decided on a siege to starve the French into surrender. By this time

camera teams from Berlin had caught up with their armies, but the surviving pictures, though few and far between, show pictures of French prisoners, gun batteries, the logistic system, and personalities, like von Moltke, the Crown Prince and Bismarck. Absent from the cannon were photographs of Prussia's major military concern at the time, the guerrilla war which *francs tireurs* were waging along their lines of communication, and which the Prussians were suppressing with ruthless severity. Beato had already taken a photograph of executed Indians in 1858, and Gardner had photographed the hanging of four people implicated in the conspiracy to assassinate Lincoln in 1865. There were numerous sketches of executions in the illustrated British newspapers, but German cameramen fought shy of recording these scenes.

With the beginning of the siege of Paris, the photographic record of the Franco–Prussian War, so sketchy for the first few weeks, suddenly becomes much fuller. Paris was the centre of European

above

In late September William Howard Russell wrote in his diary, '... much excitement was caused at the outposts by the appearance of the great Captive Balloon, which rose above Paris laden with officers, who could be seen, I am told, reconnoitring the Prussian lines. What a use of the aerial machine in which so many of us mounted during the Jubilee of all Nations at the Paris Exposition!' In fact, balloons were to provide Paris with a surprisingly regular air service to the rest of France, carrying not just mail and despatches, but most famously Leon Gambetta, the new president of the republic, over the Prussian armies.

photography, second only to London in its number of photo studios. Photographers took pictures of the new armies forming, particularly the *gardes nationales*, the 300,000-strong radical militia formed from amongst the working-class districts of Paris. They also took pictures of fortifications, of gun batteries, of barricades being built in the streets, and of the hot-air balloons which were the only form of communication with the outside world. And when the German shells began crashing into the city on 5 January they recorded the destruction. Four days later from his quarters at Versailles, where he was staying with the Crown Prince's staff, Russell recorded in his diary 'Paris burning in three distinct quarters . . . It was a calm, frosty night – moon shining, stars bright – lights in the windows of Versailles – noise of laughter and tinkling glasses. What a contrast to the tortured city beyond!'

above

A Barricade in the Place Vendome March 1871. With the establishment of the Commune, each district began setting up local defences, as had been done in the revolutions of 1789, 1830 and 1848. The defences varied enormously in sophistication, but were usually a barricade thrown across a street. The barricade at the Place Vendome consisted of a wall of cobblestones dug up from the street, effective against rifle fire, but not against artillery fired at point-blank range. The *gardes nationales* pose proudly with one of the guns dragged from Place Wagram before the Prussians entered the city.

right

The *gardes nationales* posing with a 12-pounder cannon on La Butte Montmartre in April 1871. On the surrender of Paris on 28 January 1871, the garrison's guns had been dragged to the Place Wagram for decommissioning. Just before the Prussians entered the city, the radical *gardes nationales* seized many of the guns, and dragging them to various strategic sites around the city, declared that they no longer recognised the authority of the Third Republic. Eighty-five guns were taken to Montmartre, making it a potentially strong position, but they were allowed to deteriorate and Montmartre fell easily to regular French troops on 27 May.

'THE REIGN OF TERROR' – THE PARIS COMMUNE, 18 MARCH–28 MAY 1871

Paris capitulated on 28 January 1871, and on 1 March 30,000 troops of the new German Empire, the Second Reich, marched in a triumphal procession along the Champs-Elysées. A German photographer, positioned in the Luxembourg Palace, caught the imposing scene as horse artillery and infantry lined up in the Luxembourg Gardens, before beginning the parade. Russell didn't enjoy the day. He had been seen in the company of Prussian officers, and when he left them to make his way to the Gare du Nord to catch a train for Calais to send his story to London he was accosted by bands of angry Parisians. Though very much *persona non grata* in the French capital, Russell returned to Paris to watch the Prussians withdraw.

Just two weeks later, on 18 March, the radical *gardes nationales* declared that they no longer recognised the authority of the Third Republic, and established a new form of government, a union of the various Paris communes, a Communard republic. There now followed a Communard reign of terror, in which enemies of the people, government officials, priests, police officers and so on, were tried before revolutionary tribunals and executed by firing squads. Because these events were dramatic and predictable, Parisian photographers took scores of pictures of firing squads and their victims, building on the pioneering work of Beato and Gardner. When the regular army of the Third Republic, re-armed and released from German internment, fought its way back into Paris between 21 and 28 May, the Communards burnt down the Hotel de Ville and other prominent buildings, all of which was captured on photographic plates. The French army then exacted vengeance on the Communards, using photographs of the firing squads to identify the guilty. All told, an estimated 30,000 Communards were put to death, many of whom were, in their turn, photographed before, during and after execution.

THE BULGARIAN ATROCITIES – THE LIMITATIONS OF THE CAMERA

In September 1875 simmering resentment against Turkish rule in the Balkans boiled over into open revolt in parts of Bulgaria. Suppressed by the Turks during the winter, the revolt flared again in April 1876, and this time the Turks unleashed gangs of Bashi Bazouks, Kurdish and Chechnyan irregulars notorious for their cruelty. Rumours of massacres circulating in Constantinople led the *London Daily News* to commission a freelance American correspondent, Januarius Aloysius MacGahan, to go into Bulgaria to

above left

Between 21 and 28 March the Commune ended in an orgy of destruction, as the Communards determined to remove the apparatus of the old state. Among the public buildings destroyed was the Ministry Of Finance, photographed by the landscape photographer Charles Soulier. Later in the year Soulier published a collection of his photographs of the destruction of the public buildings in the city, 'Paris Incendies', which was soon followed by the collected works of another photographer, A. Liebert's, 'Les Ruines de Paris'. In the early and mid-1870s middle-class English tourists flocked to Paris to be taken on guided tours of the largest urban battle fought so far.

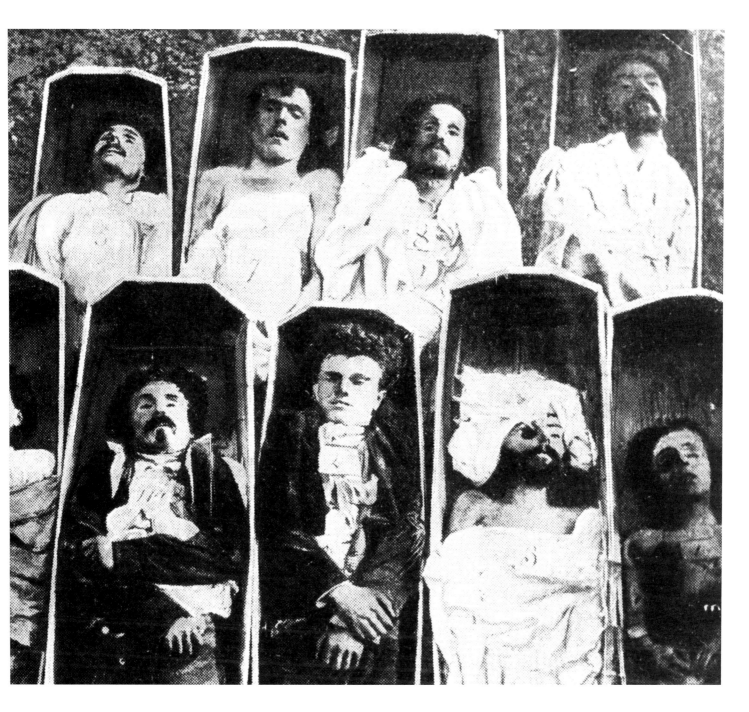

above

Some of the 30,000 Communards executed during the summer of 1871. The *gardes nationales* had expected the French regular army to make common cause with them, and were sadly disabused. Archibald Forbes, correspondent for the *Daily News*, described the scenes of horror he witnessed on a daily basis for his readers. Having caught a suspect, soldiers 'club their rifles, and bring them down on that head, or clash them into splinters in their lust for murder … They are firing into the flaccid carcass now, thronging about it like blowflies on a piece of meat. His brains spurt on my foot and splash into the gutter …'

investigate. MacGahan's despatches, published in the *Daily News*, showed that a written story was still more effective than a photograph in conveying emotion. Rather than describing the scene, MacGahan imaginatively reconstructed the events which had led up to the scene. The result was reportage of unusual force:

We were told that there were three thousand people lying in this little churchyard alone...It was a fearful sight – a sight to haunt one through life. There were little curly heads there in that festering mass, crushed down by heavy stones; little feet not as long as your finger on which the flesh was dried hard … little baby hands stretched out as if for help; babes that had died wondering at the bright gleam of sabres and the red hands of the fierce-eyed men who wielded them; children who died shrinking with fright and terror...mothers who died trying to shield their little ones with their own weak bodies, all lying there together festering in one horrid mass.

below

Photographed at the end of the Civil War as a brevet major general of volunteers, George Armstrong Custer's regular army rank was that of captain. In 1866 he was appointed lieutenant colonel of the 7th Cavalry, a substantial promotion in regular army terms, though it carried with it a salary of only 2,000 dollars, 6,000 dollars less than his salary as a major general. Like all other brevet major generals, Custer continued to be called general, but it was only a courtesy title. Much of his behaviour over the next ten years has been interpreted as an attempt to regain the security and status he had enjoyed in 1865.

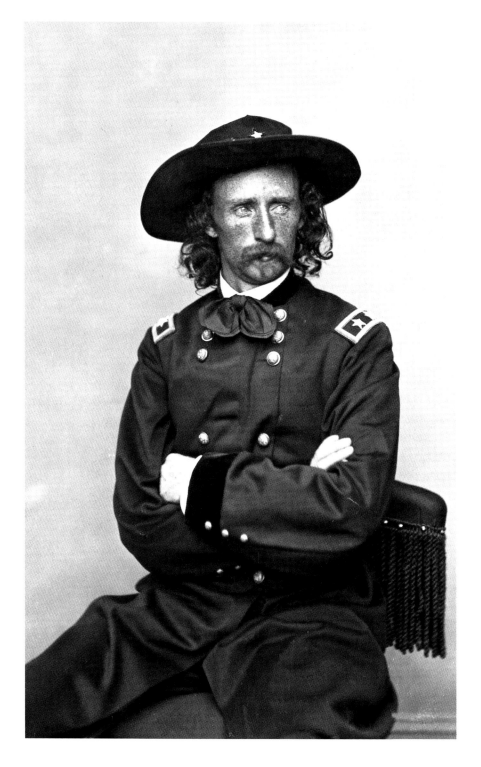

correspondents from the major Eastern papers; and a photographer, W. H. Illingworth of St Paul, Minnesota. Custer's expedition had an important political purpose: it was designed to keep Custer in the limelight with a view to a political career after the army, and it was also designed to bolster the reputation of the incumbent president, General Ulysses S. Grant, whose son, Colonel Fred Grant, accompanied the expedition as a member of Custer's staff. Illingworth took hundreds of photographs – Custer in buckskins, Custer posing by a grizzly bear he had just shot, Custer parleying with the handful of overawed Indians they encountered.

The expedition discovered traces of gold in the Black Hills, news which hit the headlines of mid-Western journals late in August. A gold rush was soon under way, with whites flooding into an area which, under the terms of a treaty signed in 1868, was a preserve of the Sioux nation. After ineffectual attempts to prevent the influx, the US Army attempted to remove the Sioux to yet another reservation, which led to the largest Native American uprising of the nineteenth century. In the early months of 1876 a number of columns under the command of General Terry slowly converged on the Sioux, now joined by the Cheyenne. After crossing the trail left by the Native Americans, Terry ordered Custer and the 7th Cavalry to ride south as fast as they could to block what he thought was the Native Americans' retreat. On 25 June on the banks of the Little Big Horn River in southern Montana, Custer discovered a long, straggling Indian village. Dividing his command into three columns, each about 200 strong, Custer rode for the centre of the village, thinking that it must hold at most a few hundred warriors. In fact some 6,000 Indian braves had camped by the river, of whom about

Illingworth's photograph of the wagons of Custer's 1874 expedition to the Black Hills, taken near the North Dakota–South Dakota border. Historians have often seen this expedition as massive overkill for the very small results it achieved in subduing hostile Native Americans, who were generally able to stay well clear of the slow-moving columns. In fact, the expedition was intended to overawe the Sioux, Cheyennes, Kiowas and others, and to make them understand that resistance to the whites was futile and that their only hope lay in seeking an accommodation. It was only when the whites violated the new treaty yet again, that the Sioux rose up in desperation.

4,000 rode out to meet him. It was all over in less than 30 minutes. Custer had a newsman with him, who died along with the others. Illingworth should have been with them, but in the summer of 1876 he was otherwise engaged. The following summer another photographer, S. J. Murrow, visited the Little Big Horn, and photographed the piles of bones which was all that was left of Custer's command.

Although the Plains Indians generally had a peculiar horror of the camera, in the American south-west the Apaches took to photographic technology with relish. After terrorising large parts of Arizona and New Mexico in the early 1880s, Geronimo, the most famous of the Apache leaders, was pleased to have his photograph taken several times during peace negotiations on 25 March 1886. Arizona's most famous photographer, C. S. Fly, took shots of Geronimo posing with his still heavily armed and not very sober war band. After his surrender, Geronimo became the centre of his own tourist industry, selling postcards of himself in various threatening demeanours for 50 cents a time.

By the late 1880s, as the Native Americans of the American West moved from being a terrifying presence to a tourist attraction, there was one last spasm of resistance. Amongst the scattered remnants on reservations there emerged a spiritual movement – a belief that if certain rituals were followed, all the warriors killed in battle with the whites would come back to life, along with the buffalo herds slaughtered to the point of extinction. Known as the 'Ghost Dance' movement, it was regarded as a significant threat by the US Army, who took steps to suppress it. Sitting Bull, the Sioux medicine man who had stirred up resistance in the mid-1870s, was killed in a skirmish on the Grand River in South Dakota on 15 December 1890. Five days later the Sioux fought their last battle, when 153 of their largest surviving war band was wiped out by the 7th Cavalry at Wounded Knee. The last gasp of Native American resistance was covered by probably the greatest of all Western correspondents, the writer-artist Frederick Remington, who sketched the Ghost Dance. It was also extensively photographed, particularly by J. C. H.. Grabill, of Deadwood, South Dakota, whose picture showed frozen Native American bodies piled into a wagon, watched by victorious cavalrymen silhouetted against the skyline.

above left
Arizona photographer C. S. Fry's picture of peace negotiations on 26 March 1886 between an Apache delegation led by Geronimo, seated centre left, and General George C. Crook, fourth from right. Geronimo's delegation included other famous Apache chiefs, Nana, Hosanna and Nachez, leader of the dreaded Chiricahuas. Unfortunately, negotiations took place near a liquor shack run by one Charles Tribolett, who sold the Native Americans large amounts of mescal and rot-gut whisky. Some of the Apache agreed to surrender, but Geronimo and all his band mounted up and rode away from the camp, screaming and swilling mescal.

The aftermath at Wounded Knee, South Dakota where on 28 December 1890 the US 7th Cavalry finally avenged the Little Big Horn. The Sioux lost 153 killed, many of them women and children, and 33 wounded. The 7th Cavalry lost 30 killed and 34 wounded, a surprisingly high total given the overwhelming strength of the cavalry's firepower, which has led historians to speculate that the majority of Army casualties were caused by over-enthusiastic troopers shooting their own comrades. With the temperature many degrees below freezing, the dead soon froze into grotesque attitudes.

'EMPIRING IT AROUND THE WORLD' – THE BRITISH EXPERIENCE

During the last 40 years of the nineteenth century, much of Asia and Africa was convulsed by conflict, as European nations transformed informal control to formal empire. Britain was foremost among the imperial nations, and British forces fought in over 30 major conflicts, which ranged from hostage rescue missions in Abyssinia, in 1867, to full-scale invasions of a country like Egypt, in 1882. The Royal Engineers had established a photographic unit in the early 1860s, but many British officers, particularly medical officers who understood the chemical processes better than most, were enthusiastic photographers. In addition, particularly in India and southern Africa, there was a growing number of commercial photographers. Together they would catalogue the expansion of empire.

After photographing the suppression of the Indian Mutiny, Felice Beato was attached to a shipment of reinforcements going to China. His mission was essentially the same as it had been on the Ganges plain – to catalogue the effect of artillery fire on fortifications. By the time Beato reached China, the Second Opium War was already in its fourth year. This war had been instigated by British attempts to impose free trade on Peking, which effectively meant defending the right of British merchants in India

to export opium to China. In August 1860 a force of 11,000 British and Indian troops and 7,000 French landed at the mouth of the Peiho River near Tientsin, the port for Peking. Progress of the advance was blocked by the Taku forts, described by the engineers as formidable 'redoubts, with a thick rampart heavily armed with guns and wall pieces'. The approach to the forts was over open mud flats, which the Chinese had turned into a killing ground, 'with two unfordable wet ditches, between which and the parapet sharp bamboo stakes were thickly planted, forming two belts, each about fifteen feet wide, round the fort'. It was not an easy undertaking, but on 21 August 1860, under covering fire from gunboats, the British Royal Marines and the soldiers of the 44th and 67th regiments, along with 1,500 French, stormed the fort, taking only about 400 casualties.

It was a far cry from the unsuccessful attack on the Redan just five years earlier. The attacking forces were undoubtedly skilled and ferociously brave – the British assault force earned five VCs – but Beato's pictures show that naval gunfire had had a devastating effect on the defenders, with the fortifications littered with bodies. This pattern was going to be repeated again and again during the next 40 years. Unlike the situation in India, when the British fought against soldiers they had armed and trained, they now had decisive technological and organisational advantages.

While the British were forcing yet another unequal treaty on China, a conflict of a very different sort broke out in New Zealand. The dynamics of the conflict were the same as those of the American West at that time – a land-hungry settler population dispossessing the native inhabitants. But the resistance of the Maoris was to prove more effective than that of even the most warlike of the Native Americans. In the early 1860s the British Army and colonial militias had the worst of the fighting, which was conducted in the rugged, heavily forested country of New Zealand's north island, ideal terrain for guerrilla operations. By the mid-1860s massive British reinforcements had arrived, including artillery and substantial numbers of Australian volunteer riflemen. The Maoris coped with increased British firepower by adapting their traditional pa, or fortress, to the requirements of war with an industrial power. Like the Viet Cong 100 years later, they dug deep trenches, bunkers and tunnels which allowed them to hold out against sometimes overwhelming British strength. At Orakau in 1863, for example, 300 Maoris held off 2,000 British soldiers for three days, and then escaped by charging through them into dense bush. British photographers, often medical officers, took copious pictures of the Maori fortifications and, when they negotiated an armistice, of surrendered Maoris.

Potentially the most difficult, but also the most brilliantly handled British campaign of the second half of the nineteenth century, was General Sir Robert Napier's expedition to Abyssinia in 1867. The world-wide expansion of British interests meant opening up legations in areas where European notions of diplomatic behaviour were not recognised. In 1864 Emperor Theodore of Ethiopia seized the British delegation and, despite protests and attempts at negotiation, refused to release them. Napier's expedition was a hostage rescue operation, and Napier, an engineer, was well placed to utilise all the advantages superior technology had conferred on Britain. The expedition's chief cameraman, Sergeant Harrold of the Royal Engineers, recorded the creation of an immense supply base on the coast, and the construction of a railway inland, which considerably reduced logistic difficulties. When the going became too rugged, Napier abandoned the technology of the nineteenth century, and used Indian elephants to haul artillery

below
Because they didn't have enough European troops to
invade Zululand, the British raised 7,000 auxiliaries
amongst the Xhosa people of southern Natal, inveterate
enemies of the Zulu. The auxiliaries were given rifles and
ammunition, and a red cloth headband to distinguish
them from the enemy tribe. On 22 January at
Isandhlwana, while some auxiliaries stood and fought,
the majority removed their headbands and either ran
away or attempted to merge with the attacking Zulus.

and ammunition, which had a considerable effect on the Ethiopians. With the British inexorably approaching Magdala, his capital, Theodore launched his warriors at them, saw them mown down by the aimed fire of Enfield rifles, and committed suicide. The expedition was astonishingly successful – even the hostages were released unharmed – and Sergeant Harrold managed to record much of it in temperatures and atmospheric conditions which would have defeated Fenton just 12 years earlier.

When the British treated their enemies with respect and utilised their technological and organisational advantages to full effect, the result was usually success. But apparently effortless superiority could breed complacency, and in January 1879 a British task force paid the price at Isandhlwanda, on the Natal Zululand border. The conflict had been the result of yet another aspect of imperial expansion, the need to provide security for Natal, a colony of European settlement, from a militarily powerful Zulu kingdom. Like Custer two and a half years earlier, the British commander separated his invasion force into three columns, and then divided his central column in two, leaving a 1,600-man force camped at the base of a high kopje named Isandhlwanda, while he took the bulk of the force off in search of the Zulus. At about 11.00 hours on 22 January, the Zulu main army attacked and overwhelmed the camp, killing virtually all the British. The disaster was redeemed only by the

right

On 11 July 1882 an Anglo–French naval task force of 13 warships began a two-day bombardment of the forts which protected Alexandria harbour. Luigi Fiorillo, an Italian photographer resident in Alexandria, took pictures of entire residential districts completely razed by giant naval shells, which the British government tried to pass off (not very convincingly) as the product of Egyptian rioters.

unable to propose a toast wishing Cavagnari well. Roberts wrote, 'I was so thoroughly depressed, and my mind was filled with such gloomy forebodings as to the fate of these fine fellows, that I could not utter a word.'

Roberts was right. News that the mission had been murdered reached Simla on 5 September. Sweeping aside Afghan resistance, Roberts returned to Kabul at the head of 10,000 avenging British soldiers, and smashed an attempt by 100,000 Afghans to overrun him on 23 December. In the following summer, after the remnants of a detached column which had been all but wiped out at Maiwand managed to fight its way back to the temporary safety of Khandahar, Roberts marched to their rescue. The march from Kabul to Khandahar, 313 miles in blazing summer temperatures in just 22 days, became an epic of the Victorian Army. On 1 September 1880 Roberts once again defeated the Afghans, and then imposed upon them a ruler favoured by the British. Burke had accompanied the army, recording the campaign in images of startling detail. Reinforcing newspaper reports, Burke's photographs, reproduced as woodcuts in illustrated British journals, helped turn Roberts into a military superstar. In one of the photographs, widely reproduced as a postcard, a calm and unruffled Roberts, exuding an air of unquestioned authority, sits alone amongst a large group of ferocious-looking Afghan tribal leaders. Roberts understood the power of the technology better than many contemporaries and, throughout his later campaigns, pursued what would today be called a media policy.

Two years later the British obsession with the security of India led to another military operation. This time it was in Egypt, where nationalist uprisings threatened the smooth operation of the newly built Suez Canal, now widely seen as the jugular of the empire. In mid-July 1882 photographers of the Royal Engineers recorded the destruction wrought by the British naval bombardment of the formidable forts guarding Alexandria harbour, which extended for a distance of four miles and mounted over 180 guns. The 25,000 troops who now landed constituted the largest British expeditionary force between the Crimean War and the outbreak of war in South Africa in 1899, and were commanded by General Sir Garnet Wolseley, who was rivalled in fame only by Roberts. After a daring night march across the desert, Wolseley surprised and defeated a larger Egyptian Army of nationalist leader Ahmet Arabi at Tell el Kebir. Photographers took pictures along the trenches, showing some of the 2,000 Egyptian dead. With Egypt now under British control, tourists began to arrive and, along with pictures of the Pyramids and Sphinx, took shots of the Tel el Kebir battlefield, little changed from September 1882, except that the dead were now skeletons.

above

On 4 September 1898, two days after the battle, the British army entered Khartoum and paraded in front of the ruins of Gordon's palace. The national anthems of Britain and Egypt were played, a 21-gun salute was fired, and a religious service was held which ended with 'Abide With Me', Gordon's favourite hymn. The soldiers then became tourists. Lieutenant the Hon. E. D. Loch of the Grenadier Guards snapped his brother officers hunting for souvenirs at the back of Gordon's palace, with the Union Jack and the Egyptian flag, hoisted at the ceremony, just visible above the wall.

An unforeseen consequence of the British victory, was a widespread Islamic fundamentalist uprising in the Egyptian-ruled Sudan. Forces inspired by the Sudan's spiritual leader, Mohammed Ahmed, known as the Mahdi, wiped out Egyptian armies at El Obeid and El Teb, disasters which led the British government to decide to cut its losses and order the complete evacuation of the Sudan. However, the officer ordered to organise the evacuation, the fundamentalist Christian General Charles Gordon, had other ideas. Ignoring instructions from London, Gordon allowed himself to be trapped in Khartoum, the Sudan's capital, where he and his garrison held out until 26 January 1885, when the Mahdi's forces finally broke in and massacred them all. A relief expedition under Garnet Wolseley, which reached Khartoum the following day, put about and steamed down the Nile for Egypt.

Few photographs survived of the dramatic events of 1884-85, partly because Royal Engineer camera teams perished at El Obeid and El Teb. But when the British returned to the Sudan in 1896, the situation was very different. Many officers now carried Kodak box cameras, which had been developed in the United States in the late 1880s. One particularly enthusiastic photographer, Lieutenant the Honourable E. D. Loch of the Grenadier Guards, kept his camera shutter going throughout the climactic battle of Omdurman, taking pictures of many incidents, including General Kitchener directing operations, and the Grenadier Guards waiting with fixed bayonets behind a thorn bush zariba, as the Mahedi's men rushed towards them. The slaughter was fearful – Lieutenant Winston Churchill of the 21st Lancers was appalled

'Whatever happens we have got the maxim gun, and they have not.' A photograph taken along the front of the Grenadier Guards position at Omdurman on the morning of 2 September 1898. The Grenadiers, part of 2nd Brigade, were on the extreme left of the British line, with their backs to the Nile. Positioning himself to the right front of a maxim gun manned by the Royal Irish Fusiliers, the photographer captured the moment at 06.50 a.m. when Colonel Hatton, the commander of the Grenadiers gave the order to open fire. They opened up, firing volleys by sections at a solid mass of spear-men and riflemen 2,000 yards to their front, bringing them to a dead halt 10 minutes later, while still 1,000 yards distant.

by the sight of bodies spread out as far as the eye could see – and Lieutenant Loch and other officers were ordered to carry out a count. Loch seized the opportunity to take pictures, but the Kodak camera proved unequal to the task. Using a tight focus Loch was only able to portray what looked like the result of a skirmish, not the result of 10,000 bolt-action magazine-fed rifles, Maxim machine guns and field guns firing shrapnel shells into a mass of men at point-blank range. Loch was an enthusiastic amateur; a professional photographer like Beato in the 1850s, Gardner in the 1860s or Burke in the 1870s and 80s would not have made this mistake. But the apparatus they used, of course, would not have allowed them even to have attempted the types of shots Loch was getting with a small hand-held camera. What was required to get the still-elusive action shot was for the professional photographer to begin using the small camera, even though this would mean sacrificing some quality. It was commercial pressure in the United States in the 1890s which was to bring this about.

MEXICAN CIVIL WAR 1911–14

RUSSIAN REVOLUTION 1905

FIRST BALKAN WAR 1912-13
SECOND BALKAN WAR 1913

ITALIAN-TURKISH WAR
1911–12

RUSSO-JAPANESE WAR
1904–5

BOXER REBELLION
1899–1901

BOER WAR 1899-1902

PHILIPPINE-AMERICAN WAR
1899–1905

03 The Birth of the Photo-Journalist 1898–1914

below

below
The wreckage of USS
Maine, photographed
after the American
occupation of Havana,
when engineers had
partially raised her. An
eyewitness report cabled
to New York described
the explosion as
'a volcano of fire and
showers of boats,
bodies, iron and guns',
which artists in the
Journal and *The World*
depicted as the result of
a Spanish mine. The
damage to the raised
hulk suggested an
internal cause, like the
explosion of a boiler, but
this was never properly
investigated.

WILLIAM RANDOLPH HEARST AND 'YELLOW JOURNALISM'

Although illustrated newspapers had first been produced in the early 1840s, they relied on either the sketches of artists, or on woodcut reproductions of photographs. The development of the half-tone process in the late 1880s allowed photographs to be printed directly on to a news-sheet. Various American newspapers experimented with this technique during the 1890s, a process which culminated in 1897 with the *New York Tribune* illustrating stories with photographs on a daily basis. As the *Tribune's* circulation soared, more and more papers joined in, including Joseph Pulitzer's *World* and William Randolph Hearst's *Journal*, a scandal-mongering sensation sheet that sold for a cent. Hearst's unscrupulous tactics forced other papers to follow suit, giving rise to 'yellow journalism', named after a popular comic strip character of the 1890s, the Yellow Kid.

'YOU FURNISH THE PICTURES AND I'LL FURNISH THE WAR'.

The competition created a demand for news and pictures of the news. New man-portable light-weight cameras were in general use in American newspaper offices by the mid-1890s, with journalists who were not only adept at taking pictures but typing a story to accompany the pictures. Pulitzer, Hearst and other newspaper barons knew that war sold papers, and by the mid-1890s were taking a close interest in a conflict then being waged in Cuba between nationalist guerrillas and the Spanish administration. Hearst sent Frederic Remington to Cuba to provide pictorial evidence of Spanish atrocities for the *Journal*. When Remington reported that Cuba was calm, Hearst is supposed to have cabled back 'You furnish the pictures and I'll furnish the war.' The Cuban guerrilla leader, Maximo Gomez, was also taking a close interest in American newsmen, because he realised that the fastest way to get rid of the Spanish was to encourage American intervention. Respected American correspondents like Richard Harding Davis described the Spanish execution of Cuban patriots, descriptions which were soon verified by the publication of photographs. In December 1896, for example, *Leslie's Illustrated Weekly* carried a picture showing the bodies of six Cubans lying on their backs, 'with their arms and legs bound and their bodies showing mutilation by machetes, and their faces pounded and hacked out of resemblance to anything human'.

On 15 February 1898 an explosion ripped through the American battleship *Maine*, while she lay at anchor in Havana Harbour, killing 260 of the crew, and injuring many more. American journalists descended on Havana, to photograph

below

Troops of the US 9th Infantry landing at Siboney near Santiago, 25 June 1898. Richard Harding Davis, who had landed at Daiquiri 15 miles to the East three days earlier with William Burr MacIntosh, described the scene: 'Soon the sea was dotted with rows of white boats filled with men bound about with white blanket-rolls and with muskets at all angles, and as they rose and fell on the water … the scene was strangely suggestive of a boat race, and one almost waited for the starting gun.'

what was immediately assumed to be a Spanish-inspired outrage. James H. Hare, better known as Jimmy Hare, an English-born photographer working for *Collier's Weekly*, got pictures not just of the wreckage, but of the *Maine*'s chaplain comforting the wounded and identifying the dead. Hare's pictures, and those of many others, crammed the columns of American newspapers in the spring of 1898, accompanied by blazing headlines demanding that Spain be punished for the unprovoked attack. On 25 April Congress took heed and declared war.

In all some 500 correspondents were to cover American operations in Cuba, many of whom had cameras and were photo-journalists. Burr William McIntosh, a society photographer and Broadway actor, had been about to appear in Lottie Blair Parker's 'A War Correspondent' when *Leslie's Weekly* hired him to cover the war. On 22 June as the American task force was preparing to land 17,000 troops at Daiquiri near Santiago on the south coast of Cuba, McIntosh and the other correspondents were told that they would not be allowed to accompany the landing. A few like Richard Harding Davis and Frederic Remington had managed to cultivate good relations with the task force commander, the enormously obese (he weighed 330 pounds) 63-year-old General William R. Shafter, and were allowed on to one of the boats. Not to be outdone, McIntosh tried to pass himself off as a soldier and filed onto a boat, but was quickly discovered and sent back. In desperation, McIntosh gave his camera and negatives to a soldier he had befriended, slipped over the side of the ship, and swam for the shore, about half a mile distant. Beating most of the boats, he retrieved his camera, and managed to photograph the landing.

above

On 1 July 1898 American troops attacked up Kettle Hill, a spur of the San Juan Ridge, which barred progress to Santiago. The Spanish commander, General Arsenio Linares, had placed about 1,200 troops on the ridge, who kept up a heavy fire on the Americans, slowing their advance to a crawl. Although Roosevelt's Rough Riders got most of the publicity, just as much of the fighting was done by the less glamorous 16th Infantry, photographed by *Harper's Weekly* correspondent, William Dinwidde as they deployed to attack. Richard Harding Davis, who also witnessed the attack, reflected on the difference between his memory of it, and the way it had been depicted in the picture papers, in which … 'the men are running up-hill swiftly and gallantly, in regular formation, rank after rank, with flags flying, their eyes aflame, and their hair streaming, their bayonets fixed, in long, brilliant lines, an invincible, overpowering weight in numbers. Instead of which I think the thing which impressed one the most, when our men started to cover, was that they were so few.'

Two days later McIntosh reached Las Guasimas on the road to Santiago, where there had been a clash between the Spanish and American forces, including Theodore Roosevelt's Rough Riders, composed almost entirely of the sons of New York's social elite. Here McIntosh discovered the bodies of his friend, Hamilton Fish, and another Rough Rider, roughly covered by blankets. A deeply shaken McIntosh was taking a picture when he heard laughter nearby, and saw a group of correspondents and officers, including Theodore Roosevelt, sharing a joke. McIntosh later wrote, 'I took a photograph and then another to show the distance from the two bodies. The photographs were taken with a heart filled with resentful bitterness … I felt a resentment toward certain of those men, who were joking with that boy's body lying within a few feet of them – a resentment which I never expect to be able to overcome.' McIntosh could have damaged Roosevelt's career, but decided to send only the first photograph to New York for publication. It appeared with the caption 'Rough Riders as they fell in the bloody engagement of June 24th – Hamilton Fish to the left – They died for humanity's sake.' Newspapers also juxtaposed the picture of the swaddled corpses with studio photographs of the handsome Fish, a study of youthful idealism and confidence. Fish became the first hero of the war – indeed *the* hero of the war – a symbol of the price America had paid to liberate Cuba from bondage.

Roosevelt, too, was to become a hero. On 1 July 1898 the Americans attacked Spanish positions on Kettle Hill, a spur of the San Juan Ridge, which dominated the road to Santiago. Many units were involved in the assault, but only one became famous. Mistaking Kettle Hill for San Juan Hill, Richard Harding Davis sent pictures of the first stages of the Rough Riders' attack back to the *New York Herald*, accompanied by a stirring account. 'Roosevelt, mounted high on horseback, and charging the rifle pits at a gallop and quite alone, made you feel that you would like to cheer. He wore on his sombrero a blue polka-dot handkerchief … which, as he advanced, floated out straight behind his head … No one who saw Roosevelt take that ride expected he would finish it alive.' Davis's report and photographs made clear that only Roosevelt was on horseback, but American illustrators soon depicted the Rough Riders' attack up 'San Juan' Hill as a full-bodied cavalry charge. The fact that other American units were also involved in the attack was also edited out of the popular consciousness. Now a military hero, Roosevelt was chosen for the vice-presidential slot in William McKinley's successful bid for the presidency in November 1900, and succeeded to the presidency when McKinley was assassinated in September 1901.

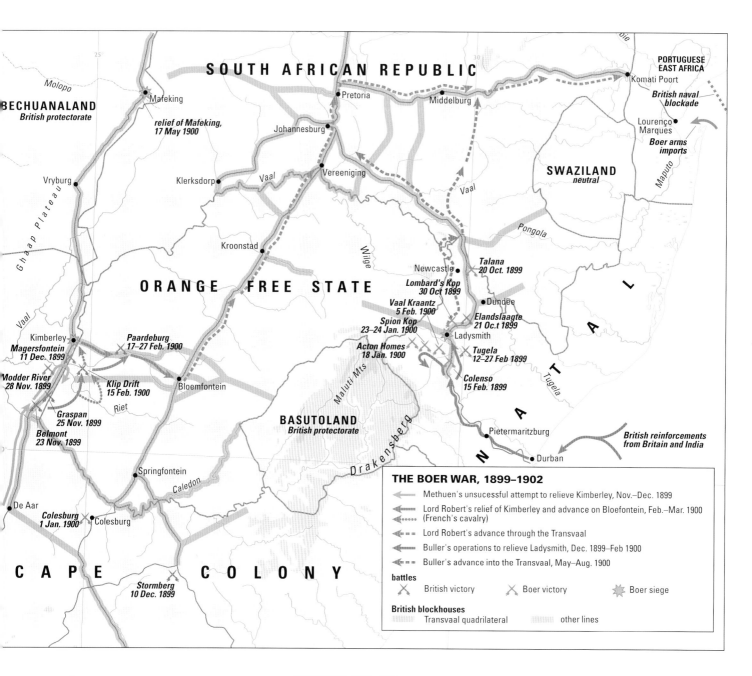

THE BOER WAR, 1899–1902

Molopo

BECHUANALAND
British protectorate

SOUTH AFRICAN REPUBLIC

Mafeking

relief of Mafeking, 17 May 1900

Pretoria Middelburg

PORTUGUESE EAST AFRICA
Komati Poort

British naval blockade

Johannesburg

Lourenço Marques

Vryburg

Klerksdorp Vereeniging

Vaal

Vaal

Boer arms imports

Maputo

SWAZILAND
neutral

Ghaap Plateau

Kroonstad

Pongola

ORANGE FREE STATE

Wilge

Newcastle

Talana 20 Oct. 1899

Lombard's Kop 30 Oct 1899

Vaal

Kimberley
Magersfontein 11 Dec. 1899

Paardeburg 17–27 Feb. 1900

Vaal Kraantz 5 Feb. 1900
Spion Kop 23–24 Jan. 1900

Dundee

Elandslaagte 21 Oc.t 1899

N

Modder River 28 Nov. 1899

Klip Drift 15 Feb. 1900

Bloemfontein

Acton Homes 18 Jan. 1900

Ladysmith

Tugela 12–27 Feb 1899

Riet

Graspan 25 Nov. 1899

Maluti Mts

Colenso 15 Feb. 1899

Tugela

A

Belmont 23 Nov. 1899

BASUTOLAND
British protectorate

Pietermaritzburg

British reinforcements from Britain and India

Springfontein

Drakensberg

Caledon

T

Durban

De Aar

Colesburg 1 Jan. 1900 Colesburg

THE BOER WAR, 1899–1902

Methuen's unsucessful attempt to relieve Kimberley, Nov.–Dec. 1899

Lord Robert's relief of Kimberley and advance on Bloefontein, Feb.–Mar. 1900 (French's cavalry)

Lord Robert's advance through the Transvaal

Buller's operations to relieve Ladysmith, Dec. 1899–Feb 1900

Buller's advance into the Transvaal, May–Aug. 1900

C A P E   **C O L O N Y**

Stormberg 10 Dec. 1899

battles

✗ British victory   ⚔ Boer victory   ✸ Boer siege

British blockhouses

Transvaal quadrilateral   other lines

above

'Marching to Pretoria.' The campaign was fought over vast distances. Initially operations centred in two areas, the north-west of Cape Colony and neighbouring areas of Bechuanaland, where the Boers besieged Kimberley and Mafeking; and the Natal–Orange Free State border, where the Boers surrounded a British force in Ladysmith. After the British broke the sieges, their forces advanced on two converging axes, one from the Cape and one from Natal, to converge on Pretoria.

BOER WAR, 1899–1902

The United States had been propelled into war with Spain as the result of a cleverly orchestrated press campaign, which asserted that it was America's duty to liberate the people of Cuba from Spanish oppression. An apparent terrorist incident, the destruction of the USS *Maine*, had provided the *casus belli*. The war was immensely popular throughout the United States, with virtually no significant opposition. When Britain went to war with the Boer republics of the Orange Free State and Transvaal in South Africa in October 1899, the ostensible cause was as idealistic as that of America's conflict with Spain. Despite repeated British protests, the Boers had denied political rights to British settlers in the

Free State and the Transvaal, where they were known by the Afrikaans word 'Uitlanders' (outsiders). In fact, all classes of political opinion regarded London's concern for the Uitlander as little more than a fig-leaf to mask the real intention – for British mining and banking interests to secure control of the Witwatersrand in the Transvaal, the richest reef of gold in the world. When Britain ignored the Boer republics' demand to halt military build-up in South Africa, the result was a Boer declaration of war, and an invasion of British colonies in South Africa, Natal and the Cape. The war did have considerable support in Britain and throughout Canada and Australasia, but there was also significant opposition, particularly from radical working-class movements and the newspapers they supported, such as the *Manchester Guardian* and the *Sydney Bulletin*. The mismatch in power was so great – the largest and most powerful empire the world had ever seen going to war with two republics of God-fearing Dutch farmers fielding only 80,000 men – that public opinion in Europe and in the United States quickly swung behind the underdog.

The Boers had no real appreciation of what a powerful ally they had in world public opinion, and no conscious effort was made to exploit it. A very effective media campaign did emerge, but it was more by accident than by design. By contrast, the British were well aware that the weight of world sentiment was against them, and attempted to control the flow of information by the most rigorous military censorship they had yet imposed. During October and November correspondents from France, Germany and the United States reached Pretoria, Johannesburg and Bloemfontein from Lourenco Marques in the Portuguese colony of Mozambique. The Boer republics were anxious to portray themselves as proper nations, with civil servants, police forces and uniformed armies, and set up convenient photo opportunities so that this image could be broadcast to the world. The correspondents weren't interested. Their imagination was gripped by the image of the Boer farmer volunteering to defend his homeland, going to war in his homespun clothes with his horse and rifle, his body festooned with bandoleers of ammunition. Richard Harding Davis, though an Anglophile American, nevertheless felt compelled to cover the war from the viewpoint of Britain's enemies. The Boer riflemen reminded him irresistibly of the Minutemen who had assembled to defend their homes against the British in 1775, a sentiment which was widely shared, even in Britain and her colonies of settlement. The Irish–Australian journalist Arthur Lynch, who had travelled to Pretoria to cover the war for the Paris-based *Le Journal*, was so moved by the sight of the Boer riflemen preparing to do battle with the British empire, that he volunteered for service and was appointed colonel of an international company. The British hit back, publishing these pictures with captions which invited the reader to ponder the rough and uncivilised nature of the Afrikaaner. Some even suggested that students of physiognomy should study the photographs closely, with the unspoken

left
War correspondent
Winston Churchill, in
a Boer POW camp near
Pretoria in November
1899. His subsequent
escape made him a hero
and helped him win the
Bolton constituency in
the general election
of 1900.

below
On the night of 22 January 1900, British troops captured
a ridge at Spion Kop, 24 miles south-east of Ladysmith, in
the very centre of Boer positions. As the sun came up, all
hell broke loose; from their remaining positions the Boers
had clear fields of fire all along Spion Kop, turning it into
a shooting gallery. Suffering huge casualties, the British
held on throughout the 23rd, the survivors withdrawing
the following night, leaving the dead behind. British
casualties numbered more than 1,800; Boer casualties
were negligible.

implication that they would find evidence of inbreeding, or of contamination
with African blood.

For six months, from October 1899 until April 1900, the Boers astonished
the world. Their columns cut into Natal and the Cape, driving the British back,
and besieging them in Ladysmith, Kimberley and Mafeking. The Boers went
to great pains to show they were a high-technology army, encouraging
correspondents to photograph the modern French and German artillery with
which they were bombarding the British. They also made sure that the arrival
of each trainload of British prisoners at Pretoria in transit for the prison at
Waterval was fully photographed, and took pictures of disconsolate groups of
prisoners, including war correspondent Winston Churchill. And they also took
pictures of British dead. The single most evocative picture of the war was

below

Boers and British communicate via graffiti. Before abandoning a farm, the Boers had written, 'Don't forget Majuba, Boys,' a reference to a famous Boer victory over the British in 1881. 'No fear, Boers, no fear,' replied the British.

taken by a Boer cameraman on 24 January 1900, of the trenches of Spion Kop in Natal, crammed with the bodies of British soldiers who had fallen victim to superior Boer marksmanship and artillery fire.

The initial British reaction to the flood of images emerging from the Boer republics was to denounce them as fakes, or to argue that they testified to the brutal and uncivilised nature of the Boers. But as the news became ever worse, the British public, and those of Canada and Australasia, swung increasingly behind the war, as the realisation sank in that the situation was truly serious. Some of the best photographs of this period were taken not by correspondents with the Boers, but by a professional from Johannesburg, Horace H. Nicholls, who joined the British retreat to Ladysmith in Natal. Nicholls' pictures show the army trudging through pouring rain, abandoning

equipment as it went, with sick and tired men sitting by the roadside. The viewer was invited to think of earlier retreats – of Moore to Corunna in the winter of 1808-09 or of Wellington from Burgos to Portugal in December 1812 – and to remember that these were the prelude to great victories.

Over Christmas–New Year 1899–1900 reinforcements poured in from Britain and India. Throughout the empire tens of thousands of men

below

Cameramen wait at Pretoria station to snap the arrival of a trainload of British prisoners of war on their way to the camp at Watersval. Such pictures did much to lower British prestige throughout the world.

right

A few of the hundreds of British correspondents who covered the Boer War. The most famous was Rudyard Kipling, seen on the right of the photograph, whose sympathetic portrayals of Indian life had made him much more than an apologist for the British Empire. Also reporting from South Africa were a number of other prominent literary figures, including Arthur Conan Doyle, Edgar Rice Burroughs, and Andrew (Banjo) Patterson, an Australian poet and balladeer who had composed the lyrics to 'Waltzing Matilda'.

volunteered from the Imperial Yeomanry, units of mounted infantry like Roosevelt's Rough Riders, who would be able to match the mobility of Boer riflemen. In previous campaigns only the officers had their own cameras, but the arrival of thousands of middle-class volunteers, most of whom had purchased Kodaks before leaving for South Africa, meant that by the end of the war Britain was going to be awash with photographs. In addition to the reinforcements, British papers sent out more than 300 correspondents, among them internationally renowned authors like Rudyard Kipling, Arthur Conan Doyle and Edgar Rice Borroughs. British papers like *Black and White* and the *Daily News* now had as many photographs as their American counterparts, while many of the British dailies published special weekly supplements of photographs of the war.

British proprietors, realising that disaster sold newspapers just as well as success, gave full coverage to British defeats like Stromberg, Magersfontein, Colenso, Spion Kop and Vaal Kranz. These setbacks, however, were balanced with an almost obsessive coverage of the three sieges, where forces continued to hold out against superior Boer forces. Papers published letters and despatches from Kimberly, Ladysmith and Mafeking on an almost daily basis, and printed photographs connected with the sieges, whether British or Boer, as soon as they arrived in England. Thus pictures of 'Long Tom', a heavy Boer gun which bombarded Mafeking, appeared in newspapers and then on postcards, achieving an almost iconic status. As relieving forces began to advance, editors cleverly suggested that they might arrive too late, thus building up enormous tension in a public who had achieved mass literacy only in the preceding twenty years, and who were still relatively unsophisticated in the face of media manipulation. The relief of Kimberley on 15 February, and of Ladysmith two weeks later, produced widespread demonstrations of patriotic enthusiasm. In Mafeking the commander, Colonel Baden Powell, sent out reassuring

messages as to the ineffectiveness of Boer shelling, which the British public, already aware of the power
of Boer artillery, chose to believe were stiff-upper-lip understatement. When news of the relief of
Mafeking reached Britain on 19 May, the country was convulsed with an explosion of rejoicing which
went on for five days, far eclipsing the demonstrations which greeted victories in 1918, 1945 and 1982.

As in all previous wars, photographers tried for action shots, and sometimes managed to get pictures
of troops about to go into battle. Much of combat, however, was conducted at ranges of a third of a mile
and more. There were many pictures of guns firing, and of shells detonating in the far distance, and
occasionally there were pictures of the results. On 28 February 1900, for example, British cameramen
photographed the wreckage of the Transvaal General Piet Cronje's encampment at Paardeberg, which
had been shelled into surrender over the previous eight days. The British wanted the world to know that
they were winning. After the initial disasters, Britain had sent Field Marshal Lord Roberts to command
its forces, with General Kitchener as his chief of staff. Roberts, whose reputation had been made in
Afghanistan 20 years earlier, understood the power of the photograph. He delayed the victory parade
following the capture of Bloemfontein in mid-March 1900 until an army of newsmen with dozens of
cameras could record the event properly. He did the same when he captured Pretoria on 5 June. With
the enemy capitals under his control Roberts decided the war was over and returned to Britain, leaving
the mopping-up operations to Kitchener.

But the war was far from over. Defeated in conventional operations, the Boer armies now broke up
into independent commandos, and began guerrilla operations against the British. In this new phase of the
war, the supply of photographs from Boer sources quickly dried up, while the British tried to photograph
a counter-insurgency campaign. In order to inhibit the Boer's mobility, the veldt was broken up by barbed
wire fences, covered at intervals of several miles by blockhouses. Columns of mounted infantry then
swept the veldt, driving the commandos into the wired and fortified zones. That, at least, was the theory.
In practice it was more difficult, with the commandos being supplied by the civilian population and
occasionally melting into it.

opposite
One of Luigi Barzini's dramatic action shots of Imperial officials beheading a Boxer. He demonstrated what was now technically possible, with a modern, relatively high-speed camera – the ability to time a shot to a split second.

below
In a scene typical of Korea in the winter of 1904–05, a Japanese official checks Jack London's credentials. Correspondents now had to cope with many restrictions, a marked contrast to the relaxed attitudes of the Americans in Cuba.

nations were outnumbered, and had to match quantity with quality. Amongst the assembled correspondents was a 26-year-old Italian, Luigi Barzini, who had just joined the staff of Italy's largest newspaper, Milan's *Corriere della Sera*. Like Jimmy Hare and Burr McIntosh, Barzini was a photo-journalist, equally adept at using the camera or the typewriter. Like his countryman Felice Beato in India 40 years earlier, Barzini recorded the suppression of a rebellion. A particularly grisly sequence – a before, during and after sequence of the beheading of a Boxer insurgent – was widely published in European papers because the executioner and the victim were both Chinese, and because it suggested that the Allies were behaving with constraint. Like Beato in India, Barzini decided to exercise self-censorship, and chose not to photograph the piles of Chinese corpses which indicated the fate of most Boxers who fell into Allied hands.

THE RUSSO-JAPANESE WAR, 1904–05

A little over three years later north-east Asia was again the centre of international attention. In its long-term search for a warm water port, the Russian empire had began to penetrate Manchuria and Korea, territories which Japan felt belonged in her sphere of influence. Sensing impending trouble, the first of some 500 newsmen began arriving in Tokyo early in 1904, while a very much smaller number hung around St Petersburg, seeking permission from the Tsarist authorities to commence the journey eastward across the almost-completed Trans-Siberian railway. Amongst the early arrivals in Japan were the veteran Richard Harding Davis, rapidly becoming the doyen of American photo-journalists, and the 28-year-old novelist Jack London, who had been hired by Hearst to report for the *New York Journal*. An improbable but very real friendship had developed between the patrician Davis, and London, who had been brought up in poverty, had been a prospector in the Klondike, and had sailed the world as a deck-hand, a background which would make him an American archetype. Davis, London and the other correspondents found themselves confined to the Imperial Hotel in Tokyo, a luxury establishment where Japanese officials could keep an eye on the correspondents and control the flow of information. Many were prepared to accept this pleasant confinement, at least initially, but London knew that his future employment depended on getting the photographs and the story that the *Journal* demanded. He slipped away, attempting to get a passage to Korea, and was arrested while taking photographs of the movement of troops to ports in western Japan.

London had found his story – he had witnessed Japan's preparations for the surprise attack on the Russian naval base of Port Arthur which took place on 8 February – but he could do little with it. Richard Harding Davis used his influence in Tokyo to secure London's release, and, of equal importance, to

right

Japanese forces suffered terrible casualties in frontal assaults on Russian positions, defended with sandbags, barbed wire and machine-guns. Not wishing to recognise the might of modern defensive fire-power, some western observers explained Japan's failure as the 'Asiatic's want of pluck'.

get the Japanese to return London's camera, though the film had been confiscated. With the other correspondents still confined to Tokyo, a few weeks later London hired a junk which he himself sailed up the western coast of Korea to Inchon, where he joined up with General Tamesada Kuroki's First Army, which was advancing northwards to Manchuria. Arrested once again thanks to the machinations of jealous rivals in Tokyo but soon released, on 1 May 1904 London covered Kuroki's crushing victory over a much smaller Russian army on the Yalu River, the border between Korea and Manchuria. London's photographs, despatched via Tokyo and published in the *New York Journal*, were the first pictures of the conflict seen in the west. As the Japanese advanced into Manchuria, London found their censorship increasingly stifling. He had already asked Hearst to transfer him to Russia, when he got into a fist fight with a Japanese soldier, and was again arrested, this time facing a court-martial for which the penalty for a guilty verdict could be death. Richard Harding Davis again came to the rescue, asking his friend President Theodore Roosevelt to intervene directly. The Japanese quickly released London, but on condition that he leave Japan and its territories.

Jack London's experiences were extreme, but the frustrations he experienced were universal. Correspondents rubbed up against Japanese censorship on a daily basis, and one by one they shipped out, some to attempt the long journey through the Tsar's empire to get the Russian side of the war. By 1905 virtually the only foreign correspondent who remained with the Japanese was Luigi Barzini, who became increasingly embedded with the Japanese armies. In March, Barzini covered almost the entire 40-mile front of Japanese positions before Mukden, where 620,000 men fought for 17 days in what was the largest battle fought up to that time in human history. Barzini took pictures of the trench systems which snaked seemingly endlessly across the rolling, open hills of central Manchuria, and photographed enormous guns firing

above

The grounded hulks of Russian cruisers, sunk by Japanese torpedo boats in their surprise attack on the Russian naval base of Port Arthur in Manchuria, on the night of 8 February 1904. A highly successful operation, it was studied intensively by the Japanese navy for more than 30 years.

from sand-bagged bunkers. He also photographed the aftermath of frontal attacks against positions protected by barbed wire and defended by machine guns, showing shell craters filled with piles of corpses. At the very point that professional military observers were writing about the importance of will-power in enabling men to advance through a curtain of fire, Barzini produced a heavily illustrated book 'The Battle of Mukden', which argued that the advantage in war now lay massively with the defence.

1905 RUSSIAN REVOLUTION

If Barzini's interpretation of the Russo–Japanese War pointed with unerring accuracy to the trench systems of November 1914, his former colleagues travelling through Russia recorded the first intimations of the convulsion which was to destroy the empire just 12 years later. The defeats at the hands of the Japanese inflamed Russian opinion, and emboldened various reformist and radical movements to demand change. On 22 January 1905 photographers outside the Winter Palace in St Petersburg caught the beginning of a demonstration of workers and their families led by Father Gapon carrying a petition to the Tsar. Other cameramen photographed the aftermath, with more than 100 bodies lying in the snow, after Cossack guards had shot them down. Riots broke out across Russia, with people venting their frustration and anger against symbols of authority or unpopular minorities. In the Ukraine mobs of peasants attacked Jewish villages, burning them to the ground, and beating to death those they could lay their hands on. These outbreaks of atavistic murder – pograms – had occurred many times before, but this

right
Some of the more than 1,000 Jews murdered in Odessa in January 1906, in a spasm of atavistic blood-letting which accompanied the revolution. Separated from the bulk of the population by religion, culture and sometimes wealth, it was all too easy for semi-literate peasants to blame all Russia's humiliations on Jewish conspiracies.

THE BIRTH OF THE PHOTO-JOURNALIST 1898–1914

time they were caught on film. In Moscow on 17 February a teenage terrorist
threw a bomb filled with nails into the carriage of the Grand Duke Sergei,
Tsar Nicholas II's uncle, as he passed through the gates of the Kremlin. The
bomb detonated, shredding the Grand Duke into hundreds of unrecognisable
pieces of flesh. The immediate aftermath was captured on film by an
American photographer who was waiting in Moscow for clearance to join
the armies in Manchuria. The most famous picture of the 1905 revolution
was of the battleship *Potemkin*, the flagship of the Black Sea fleet, the crew
of which mutinied on 17 June when they heard that the Russian fleet had
been all but destroyed in battle with the Japanese navy in the Straits of Tsu
Shima, between Korea and Japan. Other sailors followed the lead of the
Potemkin's crew, which signalled the Tsarist military and administrative
system was about to unravel. As a consequence Russia was forced to make
peace with Japan, just at the point when the land situation in Manchuria
was becoming more favourable.

ITALO–TURKISH WAR, 1911–12

The Tsar's empire was not the only one tottering towards collapse. Russia's
old enemy, the Turkish empire, was beset by national movements in Armenia,
Kurdestan, Mesopotamia, the Hejaz and the Balkans. About the only part of
Constantinople's domains which was relatively quiet was the province of
Libya, but it was here in the summer of 1911 that an assault came which set
in motion the collapse of the Ottoman empire. For 30 years a newly united
Italy had watched with growing dismay as the southern shore of the
Mediterranean was divided up between the French and British empires. The
Turkish-controlled province of Libya, wedged between French North Africa
and British-dominated Egypt, seemed ripe for the picking. Italian settlers in
Cyrenica had been abused, an Italian priest in Derna, Father Giustino, had
been murdered, and 'even the uncomplaining, fatalistic Arabs bitterly
resented the neglect and utter stagnation into which Turkey had allowed the
country to relapse', or at least so claimed Tuillio Irace, the Italian arch
apologist for annexation.

In early October 1911, after a bombardment of Tripoli, Italian forces
landed at several points along the coast, quickly securing the major towns
and cities. The Turkish commander, realising he was outgunned and
outnumbered, distributed arms to the Arab population, and withdrew his
regular forces to inland oases. Within days of landing, Italian troops were
being sniped at by guerrillas, who did not see them as liberators from Turkish
oppression. The Italians reacted vigorously. Arab suspects were rounded up

below

Greek soldiers marching out of Salonika, photographed by Walter Crawfurd Price, *The Times*' special correspondent in the Balkans. The Greeks were the best equipped and best disciplined of the armies which fought in the Balkans and, as the forefathers of European civilisation, could generally rely on sympathetic coverage from western newsmen.

opposite

The Balkan peninsula, showing the main areas of conflict. Serbian columns attacked from the north while Greek forces advanced from the south, to cut off Turkish forces in western Macedonia and Albania. Meanwhile the Bulgarian army struck into Thrace, heading for Constantinople. The Turks were saved by the Balkan League falling into disarray, giving the 'Young Turks', a revolutionary reformist party, enough time to take over the government and begin the modernisation of the army.

and executed by firing squad. Arab guerrillas hit back, attacking isolated Italian positions, and hideously mutilating the Italian dead. In Britian, the liberal newspaper proprietor William Thomas Stead, started a campaign to rouse public opinion against Italian aggression. British correspondents in Libya, Ellis Ashmead Bartlett for Reuter's, and Frances McCullagh for the *Daily News*, photographed hapless suspects being led to execution, and of the victims of Italian massacres. McCullagh questioned the accuracy of Luigi Barzini's reporting of glorious Italian victories. Comparing Barzini's account of the fighting in Tripoli with the wild and inaccurate shooting he had experienced, McCullagh wrote that 'the non-Italians who were present could hardly persuade themselves that the proceedings at which they were assisting constituted real war, and not comic opera or some Christmas pantomime of an excruciatingly funny sort.'

Barzini hit back, leading a delegation of Italian journalists into the British consulate in Tripoli, demanding that defamatory stories about Italian atrocities be officially denied by London's man on the spot. But much more effective than outright denials were accounts and photographs of Arab atrocities, if possible from British sources. Bennett Burleigh of the *Daily Telegraph*, for example, described finding five Bersaglieri who had been tied to a wall, crucified as on a cross, and afterwards riddled with bullets. Burleigh felt it was 'needless to dwell upon the nature of the further atrocities which savage Moslems invariably practise on the bodies of Christians. A sergeant had also been crucified, but with the head down, and in the hands and feet were still left enormous nails.' Like McCullagh, Burleigh backed his essay with photographs, the most shocking of which showed a soldier named Libello, of the 11th Bersaglieri, who before being crucified, had had his upper and lower eyelids perforated and laced with tightly tied coarse string. 'Each eyelid was then pulled, and the cord being pulled behind his head, the eyes were held wide open, and could neither be blinked nor closed in life or merciful death. Flies and insects abounded. The look of unutterable horror on the strained face of Libello will remain fixed forever before me.'

THE BALKAN WARS, 1912–1913

Italy had expected a quick victory, but a year after the landings found herself tied down by an increasingly vicious resistance movement. Fortunately for Italy, three Balkan nations, Bulgaria, Serbia and Greece, decided to take advantage of Turkey's preoccupation with Libya, and drive the Turks back into Asia. Turkey hurriedly made peace with Italy on 15 October 1912; two days later her armies in the Balkans faced a Bulgarian thrust into Thrace and an assault on the Vardar valley in Macedonia, with the Serbs coming from the north and the Greeks advancing from the south. A flood of correspondents descended on the Balkans. British correspondents, many of whom sympathised with Greece, went to Athens, where they photographed a smart and reasonably well-equipped Greek army marching towards Salonika. German correspondents went to Bulgaria, where the Bulgarian King Ferdinand had marked pro-German leanings. The Russians and the French went to Serbia and Macedonia, where they captured the eternal reality of war in the Balkans, the wild-looking hill men, and the Turkish irregulars, the Bashi Bazouks.

AUSTRO-HUNGARIAN
EMPIRE

• Pozarevac

S E R B I A

R O M A N I A

Vidin
Danube

Ruschuk
(Ruse)

D O B R U J A

• Balchik

Nish

• Plevna
Iskur

Shumla

• Varna

independent 1878

Novibazar

• Mitrovica

Pirot

Trnovo

B U L G A R I A

Morava

Slivnitsa

independent 1908

siege of Adrianople;
taken by Bulgarians 1912,
restored to Turkey in
Nov. 1913 by Treaty of
Bucharest

Burgas

B l a c k

MONTENEGRO

Ragusa
(Dubrovnik)

Podgorica

• Sofia

S e a

Ipek (Pec)

Küstendil

siege of Scutari

Cetinje
Lake
Scutari

Prizren

Kumanovo
23-24 Oct. 1912

Philippopolis
(Plovdiv)

Scutari

Uskūb
(Skoplje)

Maritsa

Kirk-kilisse
22 Oct.
1912

Midia

Debar

Kocani

Mesta

Adrianople
(Edirne)

Babaeski

Tchadalja
17-19 Nov.

Durazzo

Krushevo

Struma

Kirdzali

Lule Burgas
29-31 Oct. 1912

Tirana

Lake
Ohrid

Monastir
15-18 Nov. 1912

A L B A N I A

Elbasan

Lake
Prespa

Venidje Vardar
Nov. 2-3 1912

Serrai

Xanthi

Rodosto

San Stefano

Constantinople

principality 1913

Florina

Salonica

Kavalla

Dedeagach

Gallipoli

Sea

of

Mamara

Valona

Kozani

8 Nov. 1912:
Salonica capitulates
to the Greeks

Thasos
30 Oct. 1912:
occupied by Greece

Enos

Samothrace

Dardanelle

Gemlik

Argyrokastron

Imbros
30 Oct. 1912:
occupied by Greece

Bursa

Santi
Quaranta

Lemnos

Balikesir

Corfu

Epirus

Janina

Kalabaka

Larissa

Tenedos
20 Oct. 1912:
occupied by Greece

Arta

to Greece 1881

Volos

A e g e a n

Lesbos
21 Nov. 1912:
occupied by Greece

OTTOMAN

Preveza

Thessaly

Skopelos

Gediz

Manisa

Lefkas

Skyros

Chios
24 Nov. 1912:
occupied by Greece

Smyrna

G R E E C E

Euboea

S e a

EMPIRE

Cephalonia

independent 1830

Gulf of
Corinth

Patras

Piraeus • Athens

Andros

Samos

Aydin

Mendere

Denizli

Zakinthos

Peloponnese

Tripolis

Nauplia

Saronic
Gulf

C y c l a d e s

Tinos

Syros

Nikaria
17 Nov. 1912:
occupied by Greece

Mugla

Dalaman

Naxos

Cos

Santorini

Dodecanese

Simi

Fethiye

Rhodes

Milos

*occupied by
Italy 1912*

Rhodes

Scarpanto

Candia

C R E T E

*independent 1898
to Greece 1913*

M e d i t e r r a n e a n

S e a

THE BALKANS, 1912-13

—— western frontier of the Ottoman empire, 1912

position of armies, 18-20 Oct. 1912

Bulgarian		Serbian
Greek		Montenegrin
Ottoman		★ battle

areas of opposition to Ottomans at the armistice, Dec. 1912

Bulgarian	Serbian
Greek	Montenegrin

territory gained according to the 1913 Treaty of London by:

Bulgaria	Serbia
Greece	Montenegro

above

A party of Bashi Bazouks, Turkish irregulars recruited mainly in eastern Anatolia, particularly in Kurdestan. Loosely organised and poorly disciplined, they were employed on counter-insurgency operations, during which they committed countless atrocities. The armies of the Balkan League, particularly the Bulgars who had scores to settle from 1877, avenged themselves on Moslem civilians, giving the conflict in the Balkans a ferocity not seen in Europe since the mid-seventeenth century.

The greatest number of correspondents by far, however, went to Constantinople, from where they were provided with a press train to move up to the headquarters of the Turkish army. Herbert Baldwin, a British photo-journalist, took the opportunity of a delay caused by a derailment to photograph columns of Turkish refugees streaming eastward. He found 'the spectacle of silent, sad eyed women, many of them bare-footed, many carrying tiny children in their arms, plodding wearily through the mud and filth . . . a vivid reminder of what war means to the common people, the innocent victims of intrigue and maladministration.' Baldwin, who was careful to keep his camera well out of sight, avoided the fate of a less-careful colleague, who had his camera snatched from him and thrown into the mud by Turkish soldiers, furious at the insult which had been afforded Turkish womankind.

Although he had not yet realised it, Baldwin was watching the beginnings of the disintegration of the Turkish front. He later wrote that the photographer who films an attack which is successful is soon left behind; better by far to be with an army which is defeated, because the cameraman has to do very little, other than to find a vantage point on the line of retreat and begin snapping. Baldwin, who was working for the Central News Agency, and his colleague Bernard Grant, who represented the *Daily Mirror*, set themselves up overlooking a humpback bridge at Karishtiran. From here they filmed a panic-stricken mass, demoralised by Bulgarian artillery, pushing and clawing its way to safety. Most of Baldwin's shots were ruined by a technical failure, but Grant's appeared in special supplements of the *Daily News*, and confirmed British opinions about the degeneracy of the Turks. Baldwin had better luck a few days later, when he snapped a straggler who seemed to embody the whole spirit of the beaten and broken army. Baldwin recalled, 'He spoke no word, but he accepted the little food I was able to offer him with tears of gratitude that said more than any words could have done, and I felt glad that it had been in my power to help him on his way. I took a photograph of the old fellow as he resumed his journey, and I sent it home with the title "Beaten!" appended to it.' Other journalists, like the *London Daily Chronicle*'s Martin Donohoe and the *Daily Telegraph*'s Ellis Ashmead Bartlett, transmitted stories which provided a context for the photographs, and created the sense in Britain that Turkey was hopelessly degenerate.

Nothing comparable emerged from the Bulgarian side. They had the services of one of the finest photo-journalists of the period, Jimmy Hare, but kept him confined to a press pool, many miles from the action. The Sofia correspondent for the Berlin *Reichspost*, Hermenegild Wagner, complained that 'the official regulations for war correspondents clearly showed how closely the Bulgarian staff had followed the Japanese precedent in imposing fetters on the journalists at the seat of war.' Wagner then listed myriad regulations and concluded that 'it was categorically forbidden to send any news that was at all worth knowing, or to take any steps by which one could get possession of any such news.' Jimmy Hare put up with it for three months, and then decided to cover the war from Serbia.

The Times' correspondent in Constantinople, Walter Crawfurd Price, was able to cover the war from both sides by remaining behind in Salonika after it fell to the Greeks on 9 November 1912, one day before the Bulgarians reached the city. A Hellenophile, Crawfurd Price heroised the Greeks, who were 'in excellent condition, happy and bright, as befits conquerors, well clothed, booted and equipped.' The great majority of the population regarded them as liberators, shouted themselves hoarse, tore the hated fez from their heads, 'and shred them to ribbons.' When they entered the city the Bulgarians behaved very differently, looting and pillaging.

By mid-November Bulgarian armies were also closing on Constantinople, where Herbert Baldwin photographed scenes of increasing panic. On 23 January 1913 the Young Turk nationalist movement, led by Enver Bey, overthrew the Sultan and vowed to fight on, though the damage was now irreparable.

Adrianople fell on 26 March, followed by Scutari on 22 April. The Great powers imposed an uneasy peace on the combatants, reducing Turkey's European possessions to the area immediately contiguous to the Dardanelles.

With Turkey gone the members of the Balkan league now fell out. Tension had reached fever pitch in Salonika where King George of Greece had been assassinated on 18 November 1912, mercifully by another Greek, though many in the city suspected a Bulgar plot. In May heavy street fighting broke out between Greek and Bulgar forces, the aftermath of which was photographed by Crawfurd Price. Joined by the Serbs, the Greeks checked the main Bulgar advances in heavy fighting in June. A month later Rumania and Turkey intervened, the Rumanians advancing on Sofia while the Turks retook Adrianople. Bulgaria eventually signed a peace treaty in Bucharest on 10 August 1913, which stripped her of virtually all the territory she had gained in the first conflict.

The war was marked by atrocities on all sides, though the Bulgars were the worst, killing Turks, Serbs and Greeks with equal enthusiasm. Photographs of destroyed towns like Serres taken by Baldwin, Crawfurd Price and others were used in the compilation of a report sponsored by the Carnegie Endowment for International Peace, which sought to use worldwide exposure to shame the combatants into adopting civilised norms, and of substituting 'justice for force in the settlement of international differences.' The journalists also reflected on the way the war was fought. Baldwin, echoing Barzini's experiences in Manchuria, had been convinced of the primacy of artillery, but Crawfurd Price felt that the war 'will ever be distinguished by the great part played by the bayonet in the various combats.' He wrote this in the spring of 1914.

PANCHO VILLA

In South Africa, Manchuria, Libya and the Balkans, photographers had been constrained by military censorship. Even in Cuba, the military sometimes withdrew co-operation. But insurgent forces and resistance fighters – whether they were Garibaldi's Red Shirts, Geronimo's Apaches, or Gomez's Cuban guerrillas – recognised that the camera could publicise their cause. In 1910 Mexico collapsed into chaos, with several armies competing for power. In the north-western state of Chihuahua a 31-year-old bandit, Pancho Villa, transformed himself into a revolutionary, and set about breaking up the vast land holdings of local *hacendados*, and parcelling them out to his followers. A charismatic figure, his movement soon grew to thousands. Always in search of publicity, on 3 January 1914 Villa signed a contract with the Mutual Film Corporation of Hollywood, which agreed to pay him 25,000 dollars and a 50 per cent royalty of the profits earned by its newsreels, in exchange for the exclusive right to film his battles. Villa agreed to fight as often as possible in daylight, his men negotiating special rates as the danger increased.

Villa's movement was soon known throughout the United States. Photo-journalist-flooded into Mexico, including Jimmy Hare and Richard Harding Davis. The man who really created Villa, however, was John Reed, a 26-year-old Harvard graduate, who was reporting for the *Metropolitan* and the *New York World*. Like hundreds of young Americans Reed joined the rebel forces and rode with them through four months of battles. In 1914 he collected his articles and essays into a single volume which he published as *Insurgent Mexico*, which imposed on Villa and his movement a Marxist consistency which it is doubtful Villa ever subscribed to.

With conflict raging along its southern border it was inevitable that the United States would be dragged into Mexico. In April, following the arrest of unarmed US sailors in Tampico, American naval and land forces shelled and occupied Vera Cruz. Worse followed two years later when Villa raided across the US border and attacked the town of Columbus in New Mexico, killing 14 soldiers and 10 civilians. On 15 March 1916, 10,000 troops under General John J. Pershing moved south of the border, and for 11 months swept

above and below
One of the most photographed revolutionaries of all times, Pancho Villa recognised the power of an image to influence attitudes. Less than 100 miles from Hollywood, it was inevitable that cameramen and revolutionaries would find each other. Villa had a large following, not just in Mexico, but in the United States. He lost much American goodwill when he raided Columbus, New Mexico on 9 March 1916, killing 14 American soldiers and ten civilians.

Chronic instability inevitably drew the United States south of the border. Following the arrest of unarmed US sailors in Tampico, the US Navy bombarded Mexico's main Caribbean port of Vera Cruz on 21 April 1914, occupying it for six months.

northern Mexico in a vain attempt to hunt Villa to earth. Pershing did all in his power to reduce Villa's influence. He imposed strict military censorship, which was designed to dry up the publicity on which Villa thrived. Though he did not have the critical terminology, Pershing realised instinctively that photographs of Villa had an iconic status. He therefore insisted that all pictures carried a large US Army Censor's stamp mark, which soon reduced their usefulness. The Army Signal Corps took its own pictures, which it released to magazines and newspapers. Though nearly caught on several occasions, Villa escaped capture, becoming a symbol both of Mexican resistance to the United States, and of radical working-class resistance to capitalism.

In the period 1898 to 1914 photo-journalism came of age. Thanks to improved cameras and newspaper-printing technology, Jimmy Hare, Burr McIntosh, Luigi Barzini, Jack London, Herbert Baldwin, John Reed and all the others are much closer to the world of the early twenty-first century than they are to the world of Roger Fenton, Felice Beato and Matthew Brady. The photo-journalist had established a distinctive culture, which was expressed in a code of conduct which verged on the swashbuckling. Like Burr McIntosh in Cuba and Jack London in Manchuria, they were prepared to go to enormous lengths and risk their lives in order to get a good picture. By 1914 distinct subdivisions had emerged in the genre of war photography. Most controversial were pictures of the dead. Gardner's artfully arranged corpses in the Harvest of Death had been superseded by piles of corpses in the trenches at Spion Kop and Mukden. Beato's understated study of the hanging of two sepoys in 1858 had given way to Barzini's before, during and after shots of the beheading of Boxers in 1900. There were also pictures of the victims of war – Boer women and children in concentration camps, long columns of refugees in the Balkans, and butchered Arabs and gruesomely tortured Italians in Libya. All these subjects would be revisited again and again in the century which lay ahead. And there was the still-elusive action shot. Pictures of the Rough Riders on Kettle Hill had come close, but between 1914 and 1918 photo-journalists were to have more than enough opportunities to get this one right as well.

04 Photographing Armageddon

JUST ANOTHER BALKAN ASSASSINATION

On 28 June 1914 the city of Sarajevo in the Austrian province of Bosnia was swarming with photo-journalists from the major Vienna papers, who had come to cover the visit of the Archduke Ferdinand, the heir apparent to the throne, and his wife Sophia. When Gavrilo Princip, an 18-year-old Bosnian Serb student, stepped out of the crowd and fired two bullets, photographers were on hand to snap his arrest. In Vienna there was outrage and demands that Serbia, widely believed to be supporting Bosnian Serb terrorists, be punished. In desperation, Serbia appealed to Tsar Nicholas II of Russia, the self-appointed protector of the Slavic people. When Austria finally declared war on Serbia on 28 July, the Tsar ordered a partial mobilisation of the Russian army, in order to fire a warning shot across Austria's bows.

OVER THE ABYSS

Until this point the Austro–Serbian dispute had seemed just another Balkan problem, but now Europe's complex alliance system was activated. On 30 July Germany demanded that Russia cease mobilisation, and sought an assurance from Russia's ally, France, that she would not mobilise. When Moscow and Paris refused to comply, Germany mobilised in accordance with her long-term strategic scheme, the Schlieffen plan, which sent her forces through Belgium to attack and defeat France, before redeploying to defeat Russia. To the astonishment and annoyance of the Kaiser, Britain responded to the invasion of Belgium by declaring war on Germany, and a little later on Austria–Hungary. Newspapers for the week 28 July to 4 August, whether in St Petersburg, Vienna, Belgrade, Berlin or Paris, carried essentially the same picture – hysterically cheering crowds seeing their differently uniformed young men off to war. Only in London was there a slightly discordant note, with a large peace rally in Trafalgar Square, which was quickly edited out of history as crowds responded to Kitchener's call for volunteers. More and more countries joined in. Some, like Turkey and Bulgaria, sided with Germany and Austria. Others, like Japan, Italy and Rumania, threw their lot in with Russia, France and Britain. The only large, powerful neutral left by 1916 was the United States, and Britain and France were doing all in their power to bring her into the war as a co-belligerent.

'THE BESTIAL HUN'

All the major powers had contingency plans for 'Armageddon', the great battle which would sort out European power politics. Bureaucratic procedures had been set up to censor the news media, and to control the access of correspondents to armies. But the war had come so suddenly that at first near chaos reigned on the battlefronts. As the Germans advanced through Belgium and northern France, British and French photographers filled the picture supplements of the daily newspapers, and of the new journals designed specifically to cover the war, with images of burning cathedrals and libraries, and stories of raped nuns and mutilated children. One enterprising American photo-journalist, UPA's William Shepherd, scoured Belgium but couldn't find atrocities. 'I offered sums of money for photographs of children whose hands had been cut off or who had been wounded or injured in other ways. I never found a first-hand Belgian atrocity story: and when I ran down the second-hand stories they all petered out.'

CONTROLLING THE PRESS

None of the belligerents was prepared to tolerate the free-wheeling style of a Jimmy Hare or Jack London. Britain, thanks to the new Secretary of War Lord Kitchener, who loathed the press, imposed truly draconian regulations. By the summer of 1915 all correspondents found themselves corralled and controlled to a near intolerable level, far worse than the limits imposed by the Japanese and Bulgarians in previous wars. Jimmy Hare, who had left Bulgaria in disgust in 1912, felt his freedom similarly curtailed in Britain three years later. He wrote that 'to so much as make a snapshot without official permission in writing means arrest.' By contrast, Germany and Austria–Hungary adopted much more press-friendly regimes, taking correspondents on regular guided tours to various battlefronts, and imposing many fewer restrictions.

THE SCHLIEFFEN THRUST

Throughout the war, the belligerents reprinted each others' pictures, sometimes with misleading captions. Late in 1914, for example, British journals showed German troops marching through Brussels, and what seemed to be Germans rounding up Belgian civilians at bayonet point. In early November a picture appeared of masses of German infantry advancing through the dust and heat haze of late August, as they attempted to march to the west of Paris to effect von Schlieffen's great battle of encirclement. British papers hinted that it had been taken by Allied soldiers, just as they opened fire. Few pictures of the retreat from Mons passed the censor, though British and French papers printed numerous photographs of Paris taxi cabs rushing reinforcements to the Allied armies to deal a major blow to the Germans on the Marne. Unsurprisingly German papers scarcely mentioned this reverse, but filled their pages with pictures showing immense numbers of Russian prisoners, proof that Tannenberg had been a mighty victory. The same images did not appear in London or Paris until late spring of 1915, when they were used as evidence of the inexhaustibility of Russian manpower.

Because photographers had increasing difficulty in getting to the scene of action, much of the early visual material concerned the home front,

below
Passed off in British magazines as a picture taken from the Allied front line, it was in fact taken by a German photographer, who wished to convey the overwhelming force of the German advance. What he showed was an increasingly ill-disciplined mass beginning to straggle in the heat and dust of a blisteringly hot August. The Schlieffen plan was predicated on the ability of German soldiers to march more than 400 miles to the west of Paris in less than six weeks, possible for regular soldiers but well beyond the capacity of the reservists who made up the bulk of the German army.

right
Life in the trenches. When the war of movement came to an end in October 1914, the belligerents occupied trenches which snaked 400 miles from the Channel to the mountains of the Franco–Swiss frontier. At first the trenches were little better than shell scrapes, and life during the first winter, particularly in low-lying Flanders, when the trenches were often waist-deep in water, was unpleasant. The trench systems became steadily more sophisticated, with drainage and underground bunkers, dug into the side of the trenches. Eventually entire underground cities were to be created, culminating in the Hindenburg Line, to which the Germans withdrew in the spring of 1917. By this time the weight of an artillery bombardment – the British alone fired 27,000 tons of high explosives on 7 April 1917, the first day of the Battle of Arras – had caused all armies to abandon continuous lines of trenches packed with men. The front lines now comprised a network of mutually supporting strong points, fairly lightly held, with much stronger reserve positions, from which counter-attacks could be launched.

particularly mobilisation and the production of munitions. France, Germany and Austria had been invaded, and all three nations devoted considerable attention to the plight of their refugees, the unfortunate inhabitants of Picardy, East Prussia and Galicia. Russia and Britain were more fortunate, so Petrograd's journals carried pictures of murdered Serbs, while British papers brimmed over with images of Belgian refugees. The week before Christmas, Scarborough and Hartlepool swarmed with correspondents, taking pictures of the damage caused by the German navy's bombardment of the towns on 16 December. This example of 'Hun frightfulness', the censors felt should not be suppressed. The same motive impelled the censors to allow maximum coverage of the damage wrought by the first Zeppelin raids at the end of January 1915.

Governments could control correspondents, but tens of thousands of soldiers, at least in the western theatre, took their own cameras on to the battlefield. All armies had regulations in place but they were unenforceable, particularly when senior officers were often the worst offenders. In Britain publications like the *Illustrated War News*, the *Daily Mirror*, the *Sphere*, and the *War Illustrated* urged soldiers to send them their pictures, and offered prizes for the best shots in a variety of categories. As the war of movement ended in October 1914, pictures of life in the trenches filled the papers. Censors were content that the public should see pictures of their soldiers suffering privations on their behalf; indeed, the worse the privations – standing knee-deep in mud in chilling autumn rain, for example – the better.

above

The Christmas Truce. On 25 December 1914 German and British troops, their inhibitions diminished by extra rations of rum and schnapps, began singing carols to each other. Soon meetings were taking place in no-man's land, scotch and brandy were exchanged, the men swapped caps and hats, took out their pocket cameras and took photographs. Contrary to later reports, the censors in Britain and Germany made no attempt to suppress news of the truce, allowing newspapers in London and Berlin to give it wide coverage throughout the first weeks of January, and even publishing the photographs. Editorials and captions in both countries said that it demonstrated the essential chivalry and humanity of their soldiers.

SOLDIER PHOTOGRAPHERS

Editors had hoped that soldiers carrying pocket cameras would flood the press with images of combat. Overall the results were disappointing. On 14 November the *War Illustrated* told its readers that '. . . modern warfare lacks much which the battlefields of the past provided. Soldiers today are fighting enemies on the continent whom they never see . . . For this reason the great mass of photographs which reach us do not show actual hostilities in progress.' But there were exceptions. Only a week later the *War Illustrated* published a picture snapped by an officer of the Royal Horse Artillery, probably during the retreat from Mons, at the very moment an enemy shell exploded by his battery. He caught some men crouching down, others being blown sideways and terrified horses rearing up and straining at their traces. In early 1915 Private F. A. Fyfe of the Royal Highland Fusiliers, a former press photographer, snapped an equally impressive shot of the British attack at Neuve Chapelle on 10 March 1915. Troops with bonnets and caps missing, their faces screwed into intense concentration, are crawling forwards through a tangle of barbed wire to a sandbagged parapet, probably the forward German trench. In the background a banner has been unfurled, probably a marker to indicate to British artillery observers the forward position of their own troops.

CHRISTMAS TRUCE

Vicarious exposure to the realities of combat could fascinate, but so too could more peaceful encounters with the enemy. In mid-January 1915 the first photographs were published of a spontaneous Christmas Day truce between British and German soldiers manning the front-line trenches. In a letter home Private J. Selby Grigg of the London Rifle Brigade, who was based near Armentières, wrote that he and some friends 'found a crowd of some 100 tommies (sic) of each nationality holding a regular mothers' meeting between the trenches. We found our enemies to be Saxons . . . I raked up some of my rusty German and chatted with them. None of them seemed to have any personal animosity against England and all said they would be jolly glad when the war was over. Turner took some snaps with his pocket camera.'

above

'End of the *Blucher*.' With a displacement of 15,500 tons, and capable of 26 knots, the *Blucher* resembled a British battle cruiser in everything but armament, her twelve 8.2-inch guns being massively outclassed by the eight 12-inch guns of the British ships. Part of Admiral Hipper's First High Seas Fleet Scouting Group, the *Blucher* had taken part in the bombardment of Scarborough and Hartlepool on 16 December 1914, in which 18 civilians had been killed and many more injured, leading to an explosion of rage in Britain. On 24 January the squadron was on its way to conduct another raid, when it was intercepted by five of Admiral David Beatty's battle-cruisers. Firing at extreme range, Beatty's ships brought the *Blucher* to a stop, while fire from the German battle-cruisers disabled Beatty's flagship, HMS *Lion*. Thanks to signalling problems, the remaining British warships failed to give chase to the fleeing Germans but closed on the *Blucher*, literally pulverizing her at very short range. Only 234 of the *Blucher*'s crew of 847 survived.

WAR AT SEA

In 1914 all great powers used photographs of their warships to symbolise their potency, which raised the problem of how to handle pictures of ships going down. On 22 September the U9 sank the cruisers *Aboukir*, *Hogue* and *Cressy* with the loss of 1,400 lives off the Dutch coast. With bodies and wreckage washed up on the North Sea coast, and German papers celebrating the success, denial wasn't an option. Instead the British reprinted German coverage, juxtaposing the pictures of German celebrations with photographs of wreckage, making the point that the Hun was just as murderous at sea as he was on land. A little over a month later, on 27 October, the new super-dreadnought *Audacious* struck a U-boat-laid mine off the coast of Ulster, and sank in full view of other warships, whose sailors lined the decks to take photographs. This time the Admiralty imposed censorship; film was confiscated, eyewitnesses reminded of the disciplinary code to which they were subject and, although rumours abounded, the secret was kept until after the armistice. On 1 November the Royal Navy lost yet more ships, two heavy cruisers sunk by the German Pacific Squadron off the coast of Chile, although this time there were no photographs.

German success at sea in the first months of the war created a demand for images which would remind the British public, and the world at large, that it was Britain who still ruled the waves. On 9 November the Australian cruiser *Sydney* trapped the German cruiser *Emden* while at anchor off South Keeling atoll in the Indian Ocean, and smashed her into scrap metal. A month later Admiral Sturdee's battlecruisers ambushed von Spee's squadron off the Falkland Islands, sinking four of his five ships. Pictures of the wreck of the *Emden* appeared in British papers in the week after Christmas, a present from the infant Royal Australian Navy to Britannia. Three weeks later a dramatic picture from the South Atlantic reached Britain, which showed the ocean filled with bobbing heads and lifeboats, the survivors of von Spee's squadron. The most dramatic picture of this period was of the heavy cruiser *Blucher* capsizing, with hundreds of her crew standing along her keel, after she had been hit 75 times by the 11-inch guns of Admiral David Beatty's battlecruisers in an action off the Dogger Bank on 24 January 1915.

GALLIPOLI AND THE ANZAC LEGEND

In the spring of 1915 Britain launched the largest
amphibious operation hitherto undertaken to
seize the Dardanelles and force Turkey from the
war. The mood was light-hearted – British
perception of Turkish power was based on their
dismal performance in the Balkan Wars. As ever,
Kitchener was opposed to allowing
photographers on the expedition. The land force
commander, General Sir Ian Hamilton, 'begged hard for Hare and Frederick
Palmer, the Americans, knowing that they would help us with the Yanks', but
to no avail. The Chief Naval Censor, Admiral Sir David Brownrigg, appealed
to Churchill, First Lord of the Admiralty, himself a former journalist. In the
teeth of Kitchener's opposition he managed to secure the appointment of
Ernest Brooks, a former *Daily Mail* photo-journalist, as an official
photographer. The Australians, too, had an official correspondent, Captain
Charles Bean, who had been a journalist with the *Sydney Morning Herald*,
and had already taken hundreds of pictures of the embarkation and training
of the First Australian Imperial Force.

The Dardanelles was a disaster. The Turks did not run away, but fought
back with determination. Six battleships were lost trying to force the straits
without land-force support. When the British and French came ashore on 25
April the Turks, now alerted, pinned them in three separate beachheads, and
counterattacked vigorously. The record, both photographic and written, did
not underplay the setbacks. Rather, it suggested heroism on a scale which suited the magnitude of the
enterprise. For example, the *River Clyde*, the British transport run ashore at Cape Hellas to give cover to
assaulting infantry, was widely hailed as a twentieth-century Trojan Horse. Aptly, the operation had
taken place only a few miles across the Dardanelles from the site of Homer's epic siege. At Anzac Cove,
Brooks and Bean captured the dominion troops clinging on to a cliff face, an evocation of courage and
resolution in the face of almost impossible circumstances. The broad-brimmed felt hats of the Anzacs
were particularly photogenic, suggesting that these men were not really soldiers, but farmers, drovers and
cattle-ranchers, men of the great outdoors, who, thanks to healthy diets and healthy living, were taller
and stronger than the urban populations of Europe. These men were in fact natural soldiers – they had
been brought up with rifles and didn't have to be bullied and drilled like Europeans – and they had
volunteered to do an unpleasant but necessary job. Pictures of the Anzacs were well received in the
United States (Americans could draw all sorts of correspondences), and in Britain by the summer of 1915
they were being captioned 'Anzac Supermen'.

Gallipoli was presented as a justified gamble but it ended many careers. The most notable was Sir Ian
Hamilton, a good soldier with an impossible task. Winston Churchill also appeared washed up following

above

Too good to be true. A heavily cropped photograph, which originally included a trench manned by Germans firing at the attacking French at point-blank range. There are two problems. First, the weight of German fire would have been so great that the French would not have got so close. Second, the angle from which the photograph was taken suggests that the camera was on a tripod. The picture was probably posed but this does not detract from its emotional power. In the cropped version the officer dies heroically at the head of his men, who continue to press home the attack. In the uncropped version, the futility of the gesture can be fully grasped. The French attack is brave, but superior German firepower has condemned it to failure.

his resignation from the Admiralty, but he fought back, redeeming himself by serving on the Western Front, and making sure he was photographed doing so. The greatest beneficiary of the Gallipoli campaign was an obscure Turkish officer who had commanded an early counter-attack against the Anzac position. Mustapha Kemal courted the press in Constantinople, was photographed time and again in various striking poses and become the best-known Turk in the west, eclipsing by far the leader of the Young Turks, Enver Pasha.

VERDUN – THE BATTLE OF ATTRITION

A little over a month after the last troops evacuated Gallipoli, France was engaged in a desperate battle of attrition with the German army at Verdun. Pictures emanating from the battlefield showed immense artillery parks, piles of munitions, and the devastation following bombardments of unprecedented violence. Pictures of the almost-obliterated outline of Fort Doumont, which was captured and recaptured many times, came to symbolise the nature of this struggle. Both nations tried for action shots, the German press publishing an extraordinary photograph of a French officer shot as he led his men in a counter-attack. It served its purpose in Germany and Austria–Hungary, but was ignored by the Allied press.

above
Ernest Brooks's widely published photograph was intended to reassure soldiers that being blinded by mustard gas was only temporary, and could be treated effectively at a dressing station. It was a sight like this in the summer of 1918 which inspired John Singer Sergeant's 'Gassed'.

above right
Frank Hurley's photograph of a shell bursting on the Westhoek Ridge during the Passchendaele Battle, greatly praised when shown in London early in 1918. In fact Hurley had super-imposed the explosion on a picture of upturned wagons, arguing that this was the only way he could convey the reality of combat.

cut through the German defences. But the land was low-lying, the heavy bombardment had smashed a drainage system constructed over centuries and then rain began to fall. The offensive literally bogged down in a sea of mud.

The second reason that it passed into the collective consciousness of the British people was that there were so many good photographers at Passchendaele. The Germans used mustard gas for the first time on 20 September. Brooks snapped a photograph of temporarily blinded men moving back to a casualty clearing station to have their eyes washed, a photograph which was to inspire the American artist John Singer Sergeant. William Rider-Rider, in peacetime a photo-journalist from the staff of the *Daily Mirror*, was selected by Lord Beaverbrook to act as Canadian official photographer and arrived in France in June 1917. Six weeks later Frank Hurley, the Australian cameraman who had filmed Shackleton's epic voyage to Antarctica, arrived in Flanders as Australian official photographer. Together, Brooks, Rider-Rider and Hurley produced images of men living and fighting in a sea of mud which were to prove iconic. Brooks and Rider-Rider were content to operate within technical constraints but Hurley railed against them. He confided to his dairy, 'None but those who have endeavoured can realise the insurmountable difficulties of portraying a modern battle by the camera. To include the event on a single negative, I have tried and tried but the results are hopeless. Everything is on such a vast scale. Figures are scattered – the atmosphere is dense with haze and smoke – shells will not burst where required – yet the whole elements of a picture are there could they but be brought together and condensed.' Hurley, who wanted to doctor photographs, better to capture the reality, clashed with Charles Bean, who wished to be true to the camera lens. Eventually Bean agreed to a small number of composites which appeared in an exhibition of Australian war photography in London in the spring of 1918.

independence of Finland
recognized Dec. 1917

return of Lenin
from exile

Petrograd
7 Nov. 1917

German drive on Petrograd
forces Bolsheviks to sign
peace treaty at Brest-Litovsk
3 Mar. 1918

Government moved
from Petrograd
Mar. 1918

Moscow
15 Nov. 1917

R U S S I A

42 Austro-German divisions
left as occupation forces exposed
to Bolshevik subversion

grain supplies from
Ukraine prevent
starvation in Vienna

GERMAN
EMPIRE

POLAND

AUSTRO-
HUNGARIAN
EMPIRE

ROMANIA

SERBIA

BULGARIA

GREECE

OTTOMAN EMPIRE

Black Sea

Sea of Azov

Caucasus

GEORGIA

right

The Eastern Theatre.
Unlike the situation in
the West, operations in
the East never solidified
into a continuous line of
trenches. The armies-
space ratio was low, and
manoeuvre was usually
possible. Most battles
were fought on long
east–west corridors
which lay to the north
and south of Poland's
Pripyet Marshes. The
southern corridor, Galicia,
saw Austro–Hungarian
and Russian armies fight
for Tarnow, Przemysl and
Lemberg, while on the
northern corridor German
and Russian forces bat-
tled for Warsaw, Brest-
Litovsk and Pinsk.
Advances of up to 200
miles were sometimes
achieved, the Russians
performing well against
the Austro–Hungarians,
but being bested by
the Germans.

THE TREATY OF BREST-LITOVSK

——— western border of Russian territory, 1914

▢ Central Powers territory in 1914

——— frontline at Armistice 15 Dec. 1917

━━━ furthest extent of Central Powers occupation, 9 Jan. 1918

▨ area of Russia occupied by Central Powers at armistice, 15 Dec. 1917

▨ area of Russia occupied by Central Powers at peace treaty, 3 Mar. 1918

▢ area of Russia independent after Dec. 1917

✊ serious Russian mutinies in Aug. 1917

● principal towns where Bolsheviks took power, Nov. 1917–Feb. 1918

THE BOLSHEVIK COUP

For the Allies the autumn and winter of 1917–18 proved the most depressing and anxious time of the entire war. The Americans were coming but their mobilisation had been delayed by the collapse of the American rail network, and massive jams at America's east coast ports. News from Russia in the later summer was increasingly patchy, though not alarming. In mid-September *The Times'* Moscow correspondent Robert Wilton was so sure nothing was about to happen that he returned to London on leave. Amazed disbelief greeted the news of 7 November 1917, that the Bolsheviks, led by Lenin, had seized the Winter Palace in Petrograd, defended only by a women's battalion. It was widely assumed that this was an urban coup which would quickly be crushed, like that of the IRB in Dublin 18 months earlier. But three western correspondents remaining in Russia, John Reed, now correspondent for *The Masses*, Philips Price of the *Manchester Guardian*, and Arthur Ransome of the *London Daily News*, all warned that this was not a coup but a deep-rooted revolution. Photographs were rare until January 1918, when pictures of the Russo–German negotiations at Brest Litovsk which were taking Russia out of the

above

'Dough-boys' of the US 23rd Infantry Regiment, 2nd Division, firing a 37mm gun in the battle of Belleau Wood, in early June 1918. This photograph, one of the most famous American photographs of the First World War, was taken by a member of the US Signals Service, whose pictures were often derided by professionals as 'wooden'. The sudden appearance of tens of thousands of fresh, enthusiastic US troops in late May 1918 came as a nasty shock to the exhausted Germans. They knew the Americans were coming, but hadn't expected they would undertake significant combat much before the autumn of 1918, or even the spring of 1919. The fact that the Americans were willing to accept huge casualties in attacking even the most formidable German positions convinced the German high command that the situation was now hopeless.

a few weeks, but the line did not break. The Germans struck again and again between April and early July, each time getting a little weaker. A year earlier General Pershing, the commander of US forces, had arrived in France with the words 'Lafayette, we have come!', a reference to the debt America owed to the Marquis de Lafayette and his French troops during their own War of Independence. Since then nearly two million Americans had arrived in France, and were anxious to get into action. On 28 May the US 1st Division attacked the Germans at Cantigny. On 30 May the US 2nd and 3rd Divisions smashed into the spearhead of the German thrust along the Marne, and held them at Chateau-Thierry and at Belleau Wood. On 9 June a Franco–American offensive held the Germans at Noyon-Montdidier, and five weeks later the US 3rd Division held them west of Reims. And then on 18 July the Allies counter-attacked, ten American divisions providing the *elan* which French formations had last seen in 1914. The Americans were not skilful – they suffered casualties on a scale not seen on the Western Front since 1916 – but this prodigality alone served to convince the Germans that their time had run out. Unlike earlier wars there were few American civilian photographers to cover their operations – Jimmy Hare, for example, was in Italy – but nearly 500 photographers of the US Army Signals Corps made up for the deficiency.

A BLACK DAY

The British, Australians and Canadians struck on 8 August at Amiens, and in the next 72 hours advanced 11 miles, overran for the first time ever a German corps headquarters, and took more than 30,000 prisoners. It was a marvellous photo opportunity, and cameramen recorded a sea of faces, arranged *en masse* to convince the Allied public that the Germans really were on the point of collapse. Ludendorf remarked in front of subordinates that 8 August was a black day for the German army. The British broke the Hindenburg

above

Published in the British press in mid-August, this photograph of German prisoners assembled at a clearing depot at Abbeville was the first of many to appear over the next two months, designed to bolster Allied morale and convince the Germans that all was truly lost. The numbers were great, but picture editors made them ever greater by reprinting small parts of the picture several times, in order to create a composite. Only the very attentive could detect that some men appear several times. Photographs of this sort created the impression that during the First World War the individual had been submerged into a great undifferentiated mass, which explained the hunger for the stories of individual heroes, whose actions did matter, like fighter-pilots, submarine commanders, and guerrilla leaders like Lawrence of Arabia.

Line at the end of September, and crossed the St Quentin Canal. One of the assault battalions celebrated this victory by posing for its own group photo perched precariously up the canal's steep cutting. On 29 October Germany, like Russia before it, collapsed into revolution. The fleet mutinied, the Kaiser fled to Holland and a provisional civilian government negotiated and signed the armistice on 11 November.

THE WAR TO END WARS?

In Allied countries there was rejoicing. Propagandists had told the armies they were fighting 'the war to end wars', and the apparent cause of war, the militarism of Prussia, seemed at an end. But fighting was going on in the streets of Berlin and other cities, as the Communist Spartacist militias battled for control with Frei Korps returning from the front. There was also a civil war in Russia, as Tsarist generals attempted to extinguish the revolution, supported by intervention forces from Britain, France, Japan and the United States. Photographers were present in Petrograd, Moscow and Berlin, taking pictures of the street fighting. The Great War was over, but there was as much as ever to cover.

CHACO WAR 1932–34

ANGLO-IRISH WAR 1919–21

FRANCO-SPANISH
OPERATIONS IN MOROCCO
1921–26

SPANISH CIVIL WAR
1936–39

RUSSIAN CIVIL WAR 1918–21

RUSSO-POLISH WAR 1919–20

BRITISH OPERATIONS
IN PALESTINE 1935–36

GREEK TURKISH WAR 1919-23

FRENCH OPERATIONS
IN SYRIA 1925–27

BRITISH OPERATIONS
IN IRAQ 1919–35

ITALIAN-ABYSSINIAN WAR
1935–39

ANGLO-AFGHAN
WAR 1919

CHINESE CIVIL WAR
AND SINO-JAPANESE
WAR 1927–39

The Golden Age, 1919–39

With the armistice, photo-journalists were free again. As though to make the point, the Moscow-based correspondent of the *Daily News* raced from Moscow to Berlin to be the first British correspondent to enter the enemy's capital. As Germany, Austria–Hungary and Turkey collapsed into revolution, the apparatus of state control disappeared, leaving the correspondent free to photograph what he liked, as long as he was willing to risk being shot. The term 'inter-war years' is a misnomer, because the 20-year hiatus between the two conflicts was anything but peaceful, and so there was much to photograph.

There was, too, a new camera. In 1925 the 35mm Leica came on the market, a compact camera with an automatic range finder, which vastly increased the possibilities of capturing a fleeting image. And there was also a seemingly limitless market for photographs. The first steps were taken in the early 1920s with the publication of *Time and Tide* in London, *Time Magazine* in New York, and in Germany the *Illustrierte Zeitungs* of Berlin and Munich. In the 1930s the format became larger, with new magazines now devoted entirely to pictures and captions. The French led the way with the foundation of *Paris Match* in 1934, followed by *Life* published in the USA in 1936 and *Picture Post* in England in 1938.

CHAOS FIRST

The journals of 1919 carried pictures of cheering crowds, returning soldiers, the surrender of the German fleet, and statesmen at conference tables. But they also traced the collapse of empires. Bolshevism, a radical social doctrine sometimes allied to resurgent nationalism, had driven many parts of the world into revolutionary fervour. In Berlin photographers captured the fighting between the radical Spartacist militias and the Frei Korps, which stopped revolution in its tracks. In Russia the West now had newsmen with the armies of intervention, but the Bolsheviks also had their own cameramen, who, despite only intermittent film supplies, managed to create a photographic record of part of the revolution. As the White Armies closed on Moscow, and the western press daily predicted the end of Bolshevik Russia, pictures of Trotsky rallying the Soviet forces became increasingly common. At this stage Trotsky, rather than Lenin, personified the revolution. Trotsky's innate military genius, and the fact that his forces were operating on classic interior lines, allowed him to defeat each of the White Armies in turn. Soviet forces then moved on Warsaw, only to be defeated by a revitalised Polish army. Dimitri Kassell, a young Bolshevik photographer, lost his camera in this campaign — a commissar smashed it over his head as he tried to take a picture of the bodies of Polish prisoners freshly murdered by the Reds. Most villages of Eastern Europe yielded equally

above

Woman and starving child in January 1921. The government had just cut the daily bread ration for workers by a third. Road blocks prevented the urban population foraging in the countryside. Commissars investigating widespread cannibalism photographed dismembered human corpses hanging in barns like sides of beef. Floyd Gibbons's poignant pictures swayed the United States to ship out 800,000 tons of food in spring and early summer, saving millions of Russians from death.

harrowing pictures since the breakdown of the distribution system had produced widespread famine. Lenin finally decided that publicity might prick the conscience of the West and produce food aid rather than armies of intervention. In 1921 the *Chicago Tribune*'s Floyd Gibbons, a one-eyed swashbuckler in the Jack London tradition sporting a piratical eye-patch, was allowed free access to most of the famine-stricken areas. Gibbons's coverage, supported by pictures of skeletal children, produced a comprehensive Anglo–American aid package, triggered equally by Lenin's announcement of the liberalisation of the Russian economy.

The Turkish empire also had disintegrated. On 15 May 1919 Greece, believing Turkey stricken, landed an army on the Anatolian coast at Smyrna, to enforce a Greek claim to the Hellenic settlements along the Aegean coast. Simultaneously Armenian columns struck into eastern Anatolia, avenging themselves on the Turkish population for the massacres of 1915–16. Assailed on all sides, a group of Turkish officers rallied around Mustapha Kemal, formed a national government, revitalised the army and struck back against the invaders. Photos of them massacring Armenians as they struck east caused a clamour for intervention in Britain and France. Film crews were too far off to capture their subsequent massacre of the Greeks when the Turks finally drove them into the sea at Smyrna. But their simultaneous campaign to drive the Greeks from Thrace was recorded by Ernest Hemingway, then acting as a roving reporter for diverse US journals.

above

Armenian civilians massacred by the Turks in autumn of 1920. It was hoped that such photos, shot by members of the Allied control commission in Armenia, could be used as evidence to indict the Turks before the new League of Nations. The fact that the Turks had got away with genocide encouraged the young Hitler to contemplate extreme solutions for the 'Jewish problem'.

right

From July 1920 to July 1921 the Black and Tans retaliated against each IRA terrorist incident. On 1 February 1921 they burned down houses in Middleton, and on 16 February they ambushed and killed eight IRA gunmen. By the summer they had reduced IRA strength by a third, forcing its gunmen to pursue 'soft' targets such as policemen's families. Critics claimed that the security forces had descended to the same moral level as the IRA.

IRELAND AGAIN

The British empire also proved vulnerable to the force of radical nationalism, which tore at both her oldest and richest possessions. In Ireland the execution of 15 of the leaders of the April 1916 uprising had created the very force the British had hoped to suppress. On 21 January 1919 Sinn Fein declared Ireland independent, and its MPs who had been elected to Westminster in the General Election of 1918 refused to take their seats in the British House of Commons. When the British refused to recognise Irish independence, the military wing of Sinn Fein, the Irish Republican Army (IRA), launched a campaign of assassination and bombing against what they regarded as an illegitimate occupation force. At first it had great success. By the spring of 1920 British rule had ceased to exist through many rural areas in the south. In County Cork, for example, the Royal Irish Constabulary abandoned 31 police stations, which were subsequently burnt down by the IRA. Aware of the problem of fighting terrorists with a conventional army, the British decided to play the IRA at its own game, raising a force of irregulars from amongst

at first, but Steer took notes and on 28 April 1937 his devastating article 'The Tragedy of Guernica' appeared in *The Times*. The Franco regime took fright, denied it had been their allies, and claimed that the town had been burnt by the Basques or the Republicans themselves, an assertion generally supported by the right wing in Britain.

Meanwhile on the battle fronts Republican armies had done surprisingly well against the much better-equipped Nationalists, and had smashed successive Italian offensives. Fearing a stalemate, Germany and Italy stepped up aid to Franco, but no such help was offered to the Republic. Simultaneously the various factions which formed the Republican movement began falling out. The first weeks of May 1937 saw Barcelona devastated by fighting between anarchists and Communists, which created fissures throughout the Republican movement. Divided and poorly equipped, the Republicans eventually accepted an understanding with the Nationalists in 1938 that all foreign forces would be repatriated. Barcelona said farewell to the International Brigade in scenes of enormous emotional intensity, because their presence had been a symbol of worldwide support, and their departure meant that the Republican cause was now doomed.

right

The final gathering of the International Brigades in Barcelona in 1938 before repatriation. About 50,000 volunteers from virtually every country in Europe, the Americas and Australasia came to fight for the Republic. Their concentration of idealism, belief and passion all too easily spilled over into fanaticism. Franco attracted fewer volunteers – only 5,000 in all – but they were equally sincere in their desire to fight against the forces of the 'anti-Christ' republic.

below
Wong Hai-sheng's pathos-laden picture of an abandoned
waif in the ruins of Shanghai railway station in August
1938. The same image, caught incidentally by a cine
camera as it panned the ruins, confirmed that the photograph was genuine, not posed. It had an immense impact
in the United States, where opinion was much more in
favour of going to war with Japan on behalf of China
than in resisting German aggression.

THE CHINA 'INCIDENT'

The Nationalists entered Barcelona on 26
January 1939, and took Madrid two months later.
By that time media attention had shifted back to
China once again. On 7 July 1937 Japan had
launched a full-scale invasion of northern China,
with heavy fighting once again in Shanghai.
Wong Hai-sheng, a Chinese newsreel
cameraman working for the Hearst chain,
captured an unforgettable image of a solitary
baby crying in the rubble of a bombed-out
Shanghai railway station. In 1938 *Life* magazine
estimated that the still Wong took at the same
time had been seen by 136,000,000 people.
Conscious of the picture's power, the Japanese
and their apologists claimed it was a fake, and
controversy has swirled around the picture ever
since. The Nationalists had their best forces in
Shanghai, but sympathetic photographers like
Edgar Snow chose to depict the battle as one of
the Chinese people fighting a sophisticated
military machine. In December the Japanese
broke Chinese resistance and surged up the
Yangtse to Nanking, where their army ran amok
in an orgy of rape, looting and murder. Western
cameramen photographed the aftermath which
shocked the world, accelerating the process by
which the Japanese came to be seen as brutal
savages, and then as something less than human.
By contrast the Chinese became for a time the
embodiment of heroic fortitude. A photograph of
a wounded Chinese soldier on the retreat from
Nanking to Hangkow, taken by Robert Capa in
1938, said it all – China was badly damaged but
she wasn't beaten. By 1939 a generation of
photographers had honed their skills in Spain and
China – they had the techniques, the technology,
the publishing outlets and, in September, they got
yet another war.

BATTLE OF THE
NORTH ATLANTIC

NORTH AFRICA

EUROPEAN THEATRE

EASTERN FRONT

CHINA

BURMA AND SINGAPORE

SOUTHEAST ASIA

PACIFIC

06 The Second World War

below

Neville Chamberlain
at Heston Airport, 20
September 1938. After
last-minute negotiations
with Hitler to avert war,
Chamberlain flew home
to a tumultuous
welcome from a huge
crowd. A retiring,
undemonstrative man,
he was so moved by the
welcome that he bran-
dished the agreement,
declaring that Hitler had
promised he had made
his last territorial
demand in Europe.
On the balcony of
Buckingham Palace
that night he famously
declared, 'I believe
this means peace
in our time.'

In the years before 1914 there had been widespread enthusiasm for war. Conversely, during the late 1930s the prospect of war was regarded with intense anxiety. The British, French and Germans expected a war to begin with devastating air raids, like those depicted in films like *Idiot's Delight* (1931) and *Things to Come* (1936), and confirmed in photographs and film from Abyssinia, Spain and China. In the autumn of 1938 Europe had seemed to stand on the brink of catastrophe over Hitler's demand that the German-speaking Sudatenland be incorporated into the Reich. At the very last minute British Prime Minister Neville Chamberlain had flown to Munich and returned with an agreement signed by Hitler, that the Sudatenland was positively the German Chancellor's last territorial demand in Europe. A picture taken at Hendon airport of the Prime Minister holding up the Munich Agreement was flashed around the world by the new technique of radiophotography. George Gallup's new polling organisation found that Chamberlain's approval rating had gone off their scale. For a short time he was the most popular leader in the world, receiving nearly 60,000 telegrams of congratulation, while the local constituency association tried on several occasions during the winter to deselect their member, the Prime Minister's greatest critic, Winston Churchill.

The following March Hitler occupied the rest of Czechoslovakia, and proceeded to make demands on Poland, namely the return to Germany of the port of Danzig and adjoining territory, which had been given to Poland under the terms of the Treaty of Versailles in 1919. Britain and France now gave guarantees of support to Poland and many other countries in Eastern Europe, but it was too late. On 23 August Germany and the USSR signed a non-aggression pact, which was taken as a signal that war was now inevitable. *Picture* magazine in both London and Berlin carried stories told in photographs of how the crisis had developed. The German view was that their nation had been saved from a Bolshevik–Jewish conspiracy

by the election of Adolph Hitler and the National Socialist Party in 1933, from which time things had started to improve. The Jews had been forced from the economy and encouraged to emigrate, unemployment had fallen, home-ownership had increased and autobahns were being built. Hitler merely wished to wipe out the stain of Versailles, and have German people living under alien rule incorporated into the Reich. Magazines like *Picture Post* in Britain had a different take. Its photograph essays showed Nazi gangs smashing Jewish shops and burning synagogues, while factories geared up for war production. Hitler's territorial moves – the remilitarisation of the Rhineland, the annexation of Austria, the occupation of Czechoslavakia and the demands on Poland all showed that Germany was bent on European – perhaps world – conquest.

Petsamo
1939–40

Murmansk

Archangel

Narvik

15 Apr. 1940
8 June 1940
17 Apr. 1940
2 May 1940
18 Apr. 1940
1 May 1940

Namsos

Trondheim

Åndalsnes

SWEDEN

N O R W A Y

FINLAND

Suomussalmi

1939–40

Karelia

Helsinki

Viipuri (Vyborg)

1940

Leningrad

German
frontlines

Dec. 1941

Moscow

Smolensk

Bergen

Oslo

9 Apr. 1940

Stockholm

ESTONIA

1940

July 1941

Sep. 1941

Riga

LATVIA

USSR

Atlantic
Ocean

North
Sea

9 Apr. 1940

DENMARK

Copenhagen

Baltic Sea

MEMEL
TERR.

LITHUANIA

1939

Königsberg

Danzig

E. PRUSSIA

Vilnius

1940

Minsk

1939

Kursk

Kiev

Kharkov

Edinburgh

GREAT
BRITAIN

Dublin

IRELAND

Liverpool
Manchester
Hull
Birmingham
Bristol Coventry
London

Plymouth

Southampton Dunkirk

*withdrawal of
British army
1 May–June
1940*

NETHERLANDS

Rotterdam

Brussels

Cologne

BELGIUM

10 May1940

Sedan

Hamburg

GERMANY

Berlin

Leipzig

Prague

BOHEMIA &
MORAVIA

Kutno

Warsaw

POLAND

Cracow

1939

1940

Paris

FRANCE

Châlons-
sur-Marne

Maginot line

Stuttgart

Munich

SLOVAKIA

Bratislava

Vienna

1940

BESSARABIA

1940

Bordeaux

Vichy
Lyon

VICHY FRANCE
**(under Vichy
government 1940–2)**

SWITZERLAND

Milan

10 June 1940

Venice

Marseilles

Genoa

*6 Apr.
1941*

HUNGARY

Budapest

*to Hungary
1940*

Zagreb

ROMANIA

Ploeşti

Bucharest

*to Bulgaria
1940*

Black Sea

Lisbon

PORTUGAL

Madrid

SPAIN

Corsica

ITALY

Rome

Sardinia

Adriatic Sea

YUGOSLAVIA

Sarajevo

Ragusa

Belgrade

ALBANIA

*Oct.
1940*

BULGARIA

Sofia

6 Apr. 1941

Istanbul

TURKEY

Gibraltar (Br.)

SP. MOROCCO

MOROCCO

*under Vichy
government
1940–2*

Mers-el-
Kebir

ALGERIA

Balearic Is

Mediterranean

Tunis

TUNISIA

Sicily

Malta
(Br.)

Sea

GREECE

Corinth

Athens

*20 May
1941*

Crete

Cyprus

Thessaloniki

THE AXIS ADVANCE, 1939–41

Axis territory, 1 Sep. 1939	Axis advances, 1939
Axis co-belligerents	Axis advances, 1940
occupied by Axis after Sep. 1939	Axis advances, 1941
Vichy France and territories	Axis airborne landings
Soviet annexed territory, 1939–41	Allied forces
neutral powers	Soviet advances, 1939–40
frontiers, 1 Sep. 1939	Allied retreat and withdrawal
	major cities severely damaged by bombing

Tripoli

*Afrika Korps
14 Feb. 1941*

Benghazi

7 Feb. 1941

Tobruk

*11 Sep.
1940*

Sidi Barrani

Alexandria

El Agheila

11 Apr. 1941

2 May 1941

LIBYA

E G Y P T
(under British occupation)

'BLITZKRIEG'

On 1 September three German Army groups, attacking from East Prussia and Slovakia, enveloped Poland and struck towards Warsaw. Two days later Britain and her Commonwealth declared war, followed by France. Unlike the *ad hoc* arrangements of 1914 the Wehrmacht, thanks to a suggestion in 1938 by the Minister of Propaganda and Public Enlightenment, Dr Joseph Goebbels, had conscripted experienced cameramen, eventually more than 1,000, into a propaganda division under Major General Hasso von Wedel. Operating in detachments which became known as Propaganda Kompanien (PK), their role was 'to influence the course of the war by psychological control of the mood at home, abroad, at the Front, and in enemy territory'. In their coverage of the Polish campaign PK photographers established the main themes of their early work. The emphasis was on the superiority of high technology – speed, power and modernity – over masses of poorly led infantry. The pictures showed JU 87B Stuka dive-bombers supporting columns of speeding tanks and half-tracks, a war in which the maintenance of momentum would bring victory without having to fight. In mid-September a correspondent for *Time* magazine coined a German word – 'Blitzkrieg' – for what he had seen, a term which the Germans soon adopted themselves, albeit unofficially.

On 17 September the USSR invaded Poland from the east, meeting the Germans on a pre-arranged demarcation line running through Brest–Litovsk. Not to be outdone by Hitler, on 30 November Stalin sent his armoured formations rolling into Finland, in what was intended to be a three-week campaign. But in a maze of lakes and forests, and against skilfully constructed positions, the Soviets met defeat after defeat. Some of the finest photographers in the world descended on Helsinki to record a classic David v. Goliath conflict. Amongst them was Carl Mydans, whose pictures of Russian corpses frozen in grotesque attitudes, and of Finnish ski troops gliding through the forests, graced the pages of *Life* magazine. The Soviets eventually crushed the Finns through sheer weight of numbers the following spring, but their performance had been inept in the extreme, something which the German high command had observed closely.

left

The End of the *Graf Spee* 17 December 1939. The arrival in Montevideo Harbour of the *Graf Spee*, pursued by British cruisers, was the news sensation of December 1939. People across South America rushed to the imminent battle scene, while a consortium of New York businessmen chartered an aircraft at £1,250 per head. But instead her commander, Captain Hans Lansdorf, sent her into the estuary of the Platte, where she was scuttled by explosive charges before watching crowds. Lansdorf then shot himself through the head.

The French and the British had been slow to get their own information ministries off the ground, and both had conscripted photographers into official photographic units, as well as having specially accredited civilian correspondents. In contrast to the dynamism of the Germans, French photographic essays were passive, concentrating on the impregnability of the Maginot Line. British coverage reassured the public that their version of the Maginot Line, their front-line air defences, were sound, though extensive coverage of the evacuation of children from urban areas was designed to make assurance double-sure. As in the First World War, the British also needed to assert their domination of the seas, particularly after some embarrassing early losses to U-boats. This came with the scuttling of the German raider *Graf Spee* in Montevideo harbour, in front of the world's press in December 1939.

In the spring of 1940 the Wehrmacht established *Signal*, its own photographic magazine. It was inspired by *Life*; but under the direction of Fritz Solm, a journalist of considerable talent, it leapt ahead in the sophistication of its layout. *Signal* was lavishly funded – its salary bill alone for 1940–41 came to two and a half million US dollars – and it printed extensively in colour. *Signal*'s editorial staff of about 15 had first call of the thousands of photographs from the PKs which passed through its offices. It was printed in virtually every European language, and had a fairly large English language edition which circulated in the United States until December 1941 and in the Irish Free State throughout the war.

Signal's photo-essays on the Norwegian campaign of April 1940 showed that the British had behaved with near-criminal ineptitude. British readers might have been tempted to dismiss this as German propaganda, but for the fact that the coverage corresponded with that of neutral American pressmen in Norway. In Britain a political storm brewed up, which swept away Neville

Queues On The Beach At Dunkirk, Late May 1940.
Published in *Picture Post* in mid-June, the caption tried
to turn the image of defeat into a triumph. 'Even on the
beaches there was discipline and order. The lines of men
continued out into the water to the ships: "No bunching,
no pushing – much more orderly even than waiting in
a theatre queue," commented one of the last men to
leave.' Troops numbering 338,226 were evacuated, but
only through the publicly unacknowledged sacrifice
of a French rear-guard.

Chamberlain and brought in Winston Churchill as Prime Minister, just in time. On 10 May 1940 the
Wehrmacht struck in the West, cleverly drawing the French 1st Army group into Belgium, while Panzer
formations struck through the Ardennes and cut north to the Channel coast at Abbeville, trapping
Anglo–French forces in a pocket along the Franco–Belgian frontier. The evacuation of a third of a million
Allied troops through Dunkirk was a major disaster, but the few photographs taken, some by soldiers
with their own cameras, others by the civilians in the small boats who had come to rescue them, were
skilfully turned by the Ministry of Information into a propaganda triumph. They showed an army cleverly
avoiding a trap as it was about to be sprung. In Paris the mood was less sanguine. The French regarded
Dunkirk as a betrayal, and although they fought well when the Germans struck west again on 9 June,
they no longer had sufficient forces to maintain a coherent front, and capitulated on 22 June.

fires under them. And then the impossible happened. On 5 December the Soviets counterattacked, and now the theme of the PKs' pictures was Germanic endurance in the face of impossible conditions against a savage Mongol enemy. People at home were soon fully involved, donating boots, rugs and furs to make up for shortfalls in German logistic planning.

Soviet coverage of the first weeks of the war was as poor as their military performance. The most spectacular pictures were obtained by Margaret Bourke White, *Life* magazine reporter, who was in the USSR doing a special feature when the Germans attacked. Prevented from leaving Moscow by the Soviet authorities who wished to keep from the world the extent of the disaster that had overwhelmed their forces, she was able to photograph German air raids on Moscow from the roof of the American embassy. A little later she was allowed to do a spread on Joseph Stalin, showing his kindly, avuncular side, which prepared the American people for the possibility of an alliance. Soviet coverage was at a discount until 7 November 1941, the twenty-fourth anniversary of the revolution, when photographers were out in force to cover a review of the arrival of fresh divisions from Siberia, a reminder of the sheer depth of Soviet strength.

Meanwhile tension between Japan and the United States had been building, over Tokyo's attempts to expand south into Indo–China at the expense of the now stricken French. In July 1941 the United States imposed an embargo on oil exports to Japan, soon joined by Britain and the Dutch government in exile, which still had control of the oil-rich Dutch East Indies. When Japan attempted to negotiate her way out of a strait-jacket, the Americans demanded that she evacuate not just Indo–China, but China as well, which was too much of a humiliation for Tokyo to stomach. During the latter part of 1941 British and American magazines carried extensive picture essays on the strength of their forces in the Pacific – the US battle-fleet at Pearl Harbor in Hawaii, the B-17 bombers beginning to reach General Douglas MacArthur's command in the Philippines, the immense fortifications of Singapore Island and the voyage of the battleship *Prince of Wales* and 'other heavy units' to the Far East to bolster British power.

END OF EMPIRE

The Japanese struck simultaneously across one quarter of the earth's surface, from the Gulf of Siam [Thailand] to Pearl Harbor, on 7–8 December 1941. In Hawaii they left much of the American battlefleet smouldering scrap-iron; in the Philippines they destroyed or damaged most of MacArthur's B-17s on the ground; and two days later their bombers sent *Prince of Wales* and *Repulse* to the bottom of the Gulf of Siam, as their troops surged remorselessly down the western coast of the Malay Peninsula. Japanese photographers recorded success upon success, their troops liberating Hong Kong, Manila and Kuala Lumpur. The shock effect produced by Japan's advance was captured in the increasingly terse telegrams that Ian Morrison, *The Times*' man in Singapore, transmitted back to London. On 26 January Morrison

below
The Luftwaffe Attacks Moscow, Summer 1941. *Life* magazine photographer Margaret Bourke White was on assignment in Russia doing a story on economic development when the Germans attacked on 22 June. She did everything in her power to get to the front, but was consistently thwarted by an extremely nervous Soviet bureaucracy, who were terrified that she would photograph what was turning into a disorderly rout. Fortunately the Germans came to her, bombing Moscow on a regular basis during the summer.

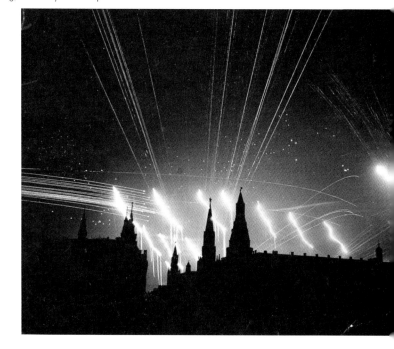

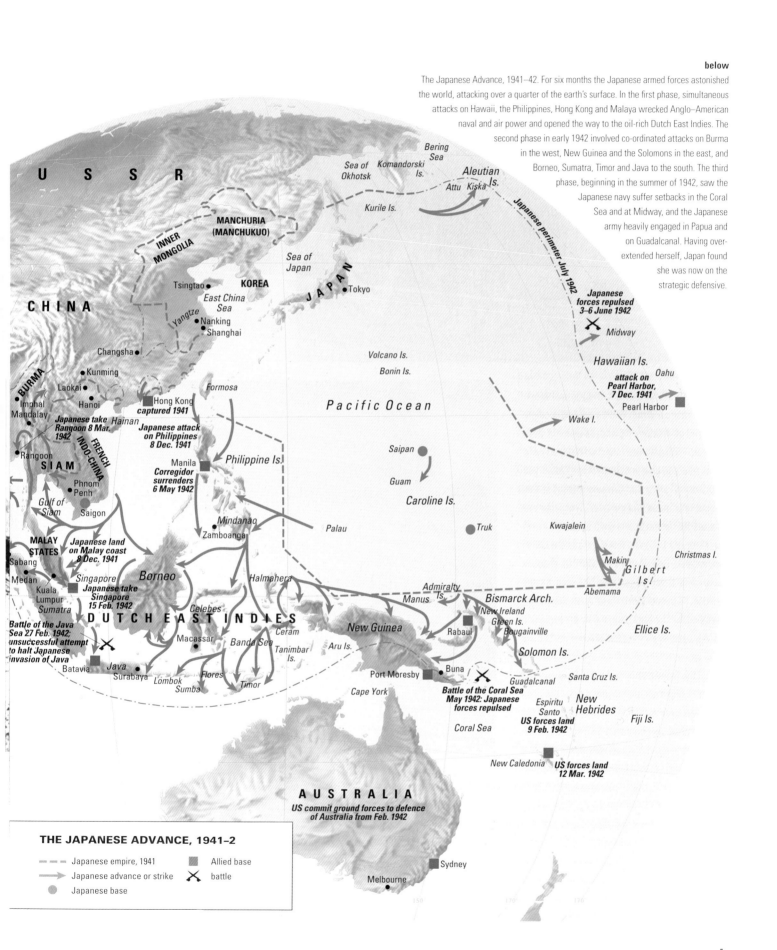

The Japanese Advance, 1941–42. For six months the Japanese armed forces astonished the world, attacking over a quarter of the earth's surface. In the first phase, simultaneous attacks on Hawaii, the Philippines, Hong Kong and Malaya wrecked Anglo–American naval and air power and opened the way to the oil-rich Dutch East Indies. The second phase in early 1942 involved co-ordinated attacks on Burma in the west, New Guinea and the Solomons in the east, and Borneo, Sumatra, Timor and Java to the south. The third phase, beginning in the summer of 1942, saw the Japanese navy suffer setbacks in the Coral Sea and at Midway, and the Japanese army heavily engaged in Papua and on Guadalcanal. Having over-extended herself, Japan found she was now on the strategic defensive.

U S S R

MANCHURIA (MANCHUKUO)

INNER MONGOLIA

Sea of Okhotsk

Komandorski Is.

Bering Sea

Aleutian Is.

Attu Kiska Is.

Kurile Is.

Japanese perimeter July 1942

CHINA

KOREA

Tsingtao

East China Sea

Sea of Japan

J A P A N

Tokyo

Yangtze

Nanking

Shanghai

Changsha

Kunming

Laokai

Hanoi

BURMA

Imphal

Mandalay

Japanese take Rangoon 8 Mar. 1942

Rangoon

SIAM

Hainan

Hong Kong captured 1941

Formosa

Japanese attack on Philippines 8 Dec. 1941

Manila

Corregidor surrenders 6 May 1942

Philippine Is.

Mindanao

Zamboanga

Palau

FRENCH INDO-CHINA

Phnom Penh

Gulf of Siam

Saigon

MALAY STATES

Sabang

Medan

Kuala Lumpur

Singapore

Japanese take Singapore 15 Feb. 1942

Japanese land on Malay coast 8 Dec. 1941

Borneo

Sumatra

Celebes

Halmahera

Macassar

Ceram

DUTCH EAST INDIES

Battle of the Java Sea 27 Feb. 1942; unsuccessful attempt to halt Japanese invasion of Java

Batavia

Java

Surabaya

Lombok

Sumba

Flores

Timor

Banda Sea

Tanimbar Is.

Aru Is.

New Guinea

Port Moresby

Buna

Cape York

Volcano Is.

Bonin Is.

Pacific Ocean

Saipan

Guam

Caroline Is.

Truk

Kwajalein

Makin

Gilbert Is.

Abemama

Admiralty Is.

Manus

Bismarck Arch.

New Ireland

Green Is.

Bougainville

Rabaul

Solomon Is.

Guadalcanal

Santa Cruz Is.

Battle of the Coral Sea May 1942: Japanese forces repulsed

Coral Sea

Espiritu Santo

US forces land 9 Feb. 1942

New Hebrides

Fiji Is.

Ellice Is.

Christmas I.

Japanese forces repulsed 3–6 June 1942

Midway

Hawaiian Is.

Oahu

attack on Pearl Harbor, 7 Dec. 1941

Pearl Harbor

Wake I.

New Caledonia

US forces land 12 Mar. 1942

AUSTRALIA

US commit ground forces to defence of Australia from Feb. 1942

Sydney

Melbourne

THE JAPANESE ADVANCE, 1941–2

- - - - Japanese empire, 1941

→ Japanese advance or strike

● Japanese base

▪ Allied base

✕ battle

THE DEFEAT OF GERMANY

- ☐ Grossdeutches Reich, 1942
- ← Axis attacks
- ←-- Axis withdrawals
- ← Allied attacks
- 🜲 major cities under heavy air attack
- ✵ major battle with date
- ✊ partisan/resistance movements
- ● commando raids
- ⦚ V1 launching sites
- ⦚ V2 launching sites
- — frontiers, 1942

Kirkenes
Petsamo
Murmansk
1944
1944
1944
1944

UNION OF
SOVIET
SOCIALIST
REPUBLICS

Archangel

Shetland Is

Orkney Is

FINLAND

1940-5

NORWAY

SWEDEN

Oslo

Stockholm

Helsinki
Narva
Leningrad
1944
Lake
Ladoga
1944
1944
Novgorod
1941-2

North
Sea

Baltic
Sea

ESTONIA

Riga
LATVIA
Velikiye Luki

Gorkiy   Volga

Dec. 1941
Rzhev   Moscow
1942-3
Vyazma
Smolensk   Tula   Kuybyshev
1941-2
Mogilev   Orel
Minsk   Bryansk   Saratov
Gomel   Kursk   Voronezh

IRELAND

GREAT
BRITAIN

Copenhagen
Flensburg
1940-4
Memel
Feb.–Apr. 1945
Kaunas
Königsberg
E. PRUSSIA
June–Aug.
1944
1944

London
1944-4
Bremen
HOLLAND   Hamburg
Sep. 1944   Lübeck
Rotterdam   Hanover
Arnhem   Berlin
June–July
1944   Düsseldorf
Calais   Antwerp   Cologne
BEL   Brussels
Cherbourg   Stettin
St. Lô   Dieppe   Dec. 1944   Rheims
Caen   Paris   Metz
1944   Frankfurt
St. Nazaire   Mannheim
1942-4   Stuttgart

GERMANY   Torgau
Oder   Stettin   Bialystok
1944   May 1945   Dresden
Prague   Warsaw
May 1945   Jan. 1945
1941-4

POLAND

Vistula

Nov.–Dec.
1943   Kharkov
Kiev   Dniepe
1942-3   UKRAINE
Lemberg   Stalino
Tarnopol   Krivoy Rog
Transnistria   1942-3

Nov. 1942–
Feb. 1943
Stalingrad

Astrakhan

Volga

Bay of
Biscay

FRANCE

Lyon

VICHY
FRANCE

Marseilles
Toulon

Aug. 1944

1943-5

Po

Milan
1944-5
Genoa
Livorno

Munich
Linz
Vienna
Apr.
1945
AUSTRIA
SWITZERLAND
Alps
Danube

Trieste

Zagreb

CROATIA

SLOVAKIA
1944

Budapest
1944-5
1945

HUNGARY

Debrecen

Jassy

Dniester

Odessa

Krivoy Rog

Rostov

Ordzhonikidze

Caucasus

1942-3

Crimea   Kerch
Sebastopol   Yalta

Batum

Black Sea

Balearic Is

Corsica

Sardinia

Rome
taken June
1944

Florence

Rimini

Jan.–March
1944
Anzio
Naples
Jan.–March
1944
Salerno
Sep. 1943

Bari
Taranto

Zara
Sarajevo
1941-4

MONTENEGRO

Kotor

ITALY

July 1943

Nov 1942

Belgrade
ROMANIA
Ploesti
Bucharest
Danube
1941-4
SERBIA
1941-4
Sofia
BULGARIA
1944

Carpathians

Mures

ALBANIA

1944

GREECE

1941-4

Istanbul

Ankara

TURKEY

SYRIA

Mediterranean
Sea

Nov. 1942
Oran   Algiers
Bougie

Bizerta
Tunis
Pantelleria

Messina
Sicily
July 1943

Sep. 1943

Oct. 1944

Athens

Aegean
Sea

Leros

Kos   Rhodes

Cyprus

IRAQ

ALGERIA

TUNISIA

April–May
1943

Feb–May 1943

Malta

Crete
1941-5

Tripoli

Benghazi

Cyrenaica

Tobruk
Bardia

LIBYA

El Agheila

Jan.–June 1942

EGYPT

23 Oct. 1942
British offensive

Alexandria
El Alamein
Cairo

Oct.–Nov. 1942

PALESTINE   LEBANON
TRANSJORDAN

SAUDI
ARABIA

The Defeat of Germany. Beginning in the autumn of 1942 Allied counter-offensives began to reduce the dimensions of Hitler's empire. While the western Allies cleared the coast of North Africa (May 1943), and struck through Sicily (July 43) and Italy (September 43), the Soviets launched major offensives after Stalingrad (February 1943) and Kursk (July 1943), which cleared much of the Ukraine and Russia. In June 1944 two almost simultaneous hammer blows hit the Germans – the western Allies landed in Normandy, while the Soviets eliminated German forces in Belorussia. Advancing from west and east, the Allies met on the Elbe on 9 April 1945, leaving pockets to the north and south which surrendered at the beginning of May, following Hitler's suicide on 30 April.

Concentration Camp Victims in Buchenwald, April 1945. Margaret Bourke White's pictures were printed around the world, along with images from Belsen, Dachau and dozens of other camps. The political impact of these pictures was immense. Resistance to the foundation of the state of Israel all but evaporated amongst non-Arab peoples. The Allies believed they had the moral authority to conduct legally questionable trials for war crimes, and nagging doubts about the ethics of incendiaries raids on German cities were buried, at least for a time.

RED STORM

In January, while the western Allies were still recovering from the German Ardennes offensive, the Soviets launched a massive attack which carried their forces across the frozen plains of Poland from the Vistula to the Oder River, at a point only about 60 miles from Berlin. While the Soviets regrouped and resupplied, the western Allies fought their way slowly to the Rhine. Helped greatly by the capture of an undemolished railway bridge at Remegan, on 21 March they crossed in strength and, after breaking through a thin crust of resistance, struck into the heart of Germany. It was here they learned about the true nature of the Nazi regime, as they stumbled across concentration camps containing the pitiful remnants of European Jewry, the survivors of the extermination camps of the east. Many harrowing pictures were taken, but Margaret Bourke White's photograph of Buchenwald has an almost cinematic horror. The Russians already knew the true nature of the Nazi regime from first-hand experience. On 16 April Zhukov and Koniev launched their offensives towards Berlin. Zhukov's initial onslaught was bloodily repulsed for three days on the Seelow Heights to the east overlooking the floodplain of the Oder, an indication that the Germans were still capable of extremely effective resistance. But Koniev's tanks, smashing in from the south-east, cracked the last defences. The Soviet thrusts met to the west of the city on 25 April, cutting it off from outside support, while infantry fought their way into the centre, street by street. On 30 April, the day Hitler killed himself, Russian soldiers climbed to the top of the Reichstag to hang a huge improvised Soviet flag over the city, a moment captured by TASS photographer Yevgeny Khaldei. In the basement the 5,000 German troops were still resisting fiercely, and would not surrender for another 48 hours, but it was vital the picture was in Moscow for the celebrations of 1 May.

The Red Flag atop the Reichs Chancellery, 1 May 1945. Ukrainian photographer Yevgeni Khaldei's dramatic shot of Soviet soldiers raising a large red flag (actually a tablecloth with a hammer and sickle sewn on) while Nazi fanatics still hold out in the basement. The photo had to be retouched before publication, because the right arm of the man supporting the flag-bearer was festooned with wrist-watches, clear evidence of looting.

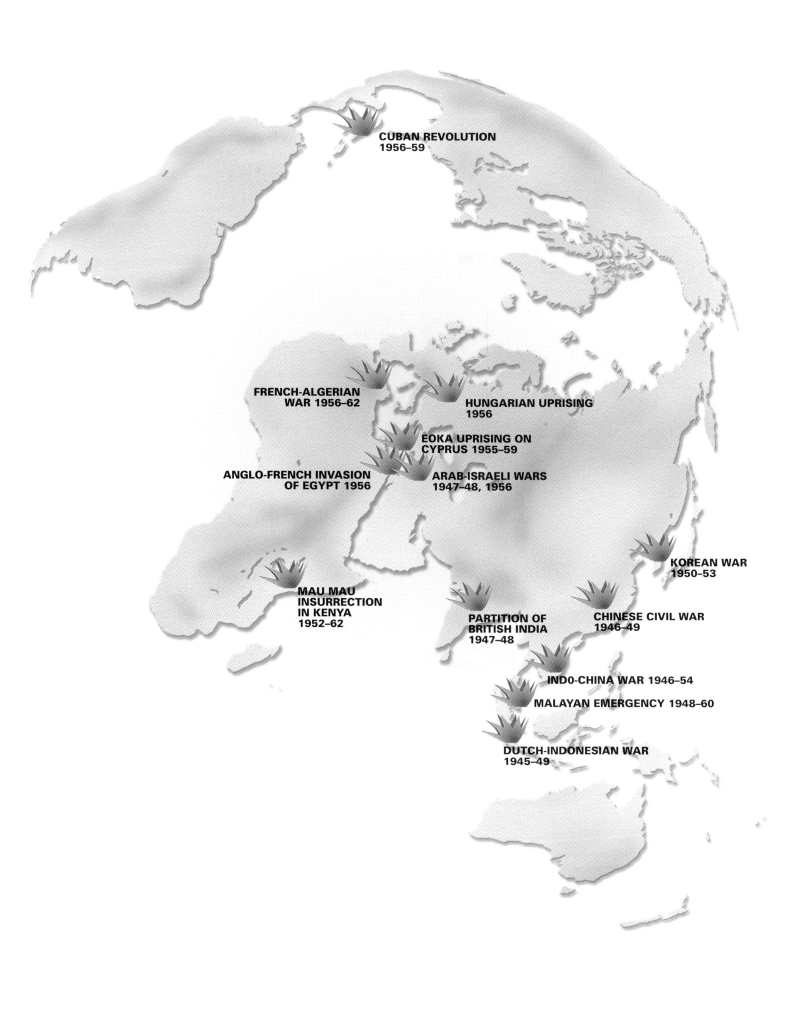

CUBAN REVOLUTION
1956–59

FRENCH-ALGERIAN
WAR 1956–62

HUNGARIAN UPRISING
1956

EOKA UPRISING ON
CYPRUS 1955–59

ANGLO-FRENCH INVASION
OF EGYPT 1956

ARAB-ISRAELI WARS
1947–48, 1956

KOREAN WAR
1950–53

MAU MAU
INSURRECTION
IN KENYA
1952–62

PARTITION OF
BRITISH INDIA
1947–48

CHINESE CIVIL WAR
1946–49

IND0-CHINA WAR 1946–54

MALAYAN EMERGENCY 1948–60

DUTCH-INDONESIAN WAR
1945–49

Hot Spots in the Cold War, 1946–64

below

The Hydrogen Bomb. Eniwetok Atoll, 1 November 1952. Equivalent to a million tons of TNT, its explosive power matched 100 conventional bomber raids of the type which destroyed Dresden. The world's first hydrogen bomb required a Hiroshima-type atomic bomb to trigger the detonation. Discovery of the long-term effects of radioactive fall-out fuelled speculation about the end of life on earth. For a generation just coming to terms with the power of the A-bomb, the H-bomb came as a profound shock. In the American mid-west, an area previously remote from the threat of war, children were taught to 'tuck and duck' to help survive the fireball. Something like a 'bomb psychosis' gripped this generation, a mindframe subsequently blamed for many forms of what was then considered aberrant behaviour, from beatniks to rock and roll.

THE BOMB

In 1945 the most important news story was the atomic bomb – a world-changing invention. Although the Americans had relied on British help to build the bomb, they secured a monopoly on it by rushing an act through Congress forbidding further collaboration. Both the British and the Soviets then raced to develop their own bombs. On 19 September 1949 an agitated President Truman announced the detection of the first Russian A-bomb test. The British finally detonated their own bomb in the Monte Bello islands off the coast of Western Australia on 3 October 1952. By this time the United States had been working on the development of a thermo-nuclear weapon, a hydrogen bomb, for two years and detonated it on Eniwetok Atoll on 1 November 1952. Equivalent to 50 times the explosion that destroyed Hiroshima, the blast atomised the island. America's lead was short-lived – on 12 August 1953 the Soviets also detonated an H-bomb. Prototypes of the American B-52 and the British Victor and Vulcan long-range bombers had already flown, and were joined in 1954 by the Soviets' long-range Tupolev TU 16 Badger Bomber. Over subsequent decades the western alliance and the Soviet bloc refined and developed increasingly sophisticated missile systems.

Many people now believed that the next war, the inevitable clash between the American and Soviet 'empires', would be an all-out nuclear war which might bring life on earth to an end. Yet analysts

gradually realised that nuclear capability might prove a deterrent, rather than a stimulus, to war. The United States and the Soviet Union would fight by proxy through client states – a so-called 'Cold War' – and if they became directly involved in a conflict, they would consciously fight well below the threshold of their capabilities. There were to be no total wars, but at any one time a dozen or so limited wars caused by the interaction of Cold War tensions with the break-up of the colonial empires.

The photo-journalists of this generation were collectively the most experienced ever to cover conflict. Most had started in Abyssinia, Spain and China ten years earlier, and had then had the six years of the Second World War to hone their skills. They were used to wearing uniforms, and having military rank and military friends. They were men and women used to exercising self-censorship, which explains the curious quality of photo-journalism during this period – technically brilliant, but with a reluctance to follow up stories that might prove embarrassing to their close officer friends.

right

In 1946 Chiang Kai-shek's nationalist forces, re-equipped by the USA, struck into Communist-controlled North China and Manchuria, where they were heavily defeated by Mao Tse-tung's armies, now equipped with Japanese tanks and heavy artillery. The final stage of the conflict in China saw huge forces engaged in massive conventional battles, with the nationalists outfought at every turn.

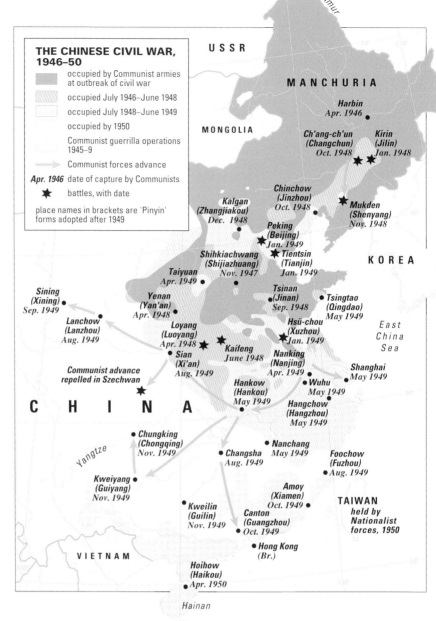

THE CHINESE CIVIL WAR, 1946–50

- occupied by Communist armies at outbreak of civil war
- occupied July 1946–June 1948
- occupied July 1948–June 1949
- occupied by 1950
- Communist guerrilla operations 1945–9
- → Communist forces advance
- *Apr. 1946* date of capture by Communists
- ★ battles, with date

place names in brackets are 'Pinyin' forms adopted after 1949

TROUBLE IN PALESTINE

But they were more than ready to investigate the activities of other armies. American journalists were fascinated by the disintegrating British Empire. AP's Max Desfor photographed massacres in the Indian subcontinent and riots in Burma. The story that got the greatest coverage was the three-sided war being waged in Palestine, where the British were endeavouring to keep Jews and Arabs from each others' throats. On 22 July 1946 the Stern Gang, a Zionist terrorist organisation, blew up the King David Hotel, British military headquarters in Jerusalem, killing 91 and injuring 56, many of whom were hideously disfigured. It was the single worst terrorist act carried out against the British army, their wives and children and was followed by more bombings, reprisals, executions and murders. Stories from the *Herald Tribune*'s Homer Bigart, and pictures by Pulitzer prizewinner Frank E. 'Pappy' Noel of Jewish girls being marched under arrest by British soldiers, and of a pitched battle fought to prevent Jewish refugees disembarking from the American-crewed *Exodus*, turned American opinion against Britain, and hastened her decision to hand her mandate over to the United Nations. When Palestine was partitioned in January 1948, six Arab armies attacked the new state of Israel. Robert Capa was on hand to record what he believed might be a second Masada, the final stand of the Israelites against the Romans in AD 73. Yet Israel triumphed, thanks to a courage born of desperation, and a poorly trained Arab army.

American attention was also focused on China. In 1945 Theodore White resigned as China

above left

Ruins of the King David Hotel, 22 July 1946. On 22 July Irgun guerrillas, disguised as Arabs, planted seven explosive-packed milk-churns in the kitchens of the King David Hotel. The death of 91 people, many of them women and children, shocked world opinion. Moderate Jews withdrew from the united resistance movement. The Irgun, with only 1,500 active members, had little alternative but to increase the level of terror. Tit-for-tat atrocities, reminiscent of Ireland in 1919–22, marked the remainder of the campaign. In July 1947, after four convicted terrorists were executed, the Irgun kidnapped and hanged two British Military Police NCOs, leaving their booby-trapped bodies swinging from orchard trees. By the time the British withdrew, the campaign in Palestine had cost 338 soldiers and civilians killed.

THE KOREAN WAR

CHINA

Chosan

Antung

Chinese intervention Oct. 1950

Iwon

Unsan

Hungnam

US airborne landings 20 Oct. 1950

NORTH KOREA

Wonsan

landing of US 7 Division, 26 Oct. 1950

Pyongyang

UN maximum advance 2 Nov. 1950 before start of Chinese counter-attack

armistice line 27 July 1953

38th Parallel

Panmunjom

Seoul

Inchon   Wonju

landing of US X Corps 15 Sep. 1950

Chinese and North Korean maximum advance 25 Jan. 1951

SOUTH KOREA

Taejon

Pohang

Taegu

North Korean maximum advance 15 Sep. 1950

Mokpo

Pusan

left

The Korean War, 1950–53. Fought in a peninsula 120 miles wide and 400 miles long, the first nine months saw rapid advances by both belligerents. The North Koreans drove south to the Pusan perimeter, and the UN counterattacked and drove the North Koreans up to the Yalu River. Chinese intervention pushed the front line south, where it stabilised for two years of attrition.

below

Communist Atrocity, July 1950. Appearing in *Newsweek* on 24 July, the caption said 'Murdered: This American prisoner with hands bound, was shot by the Reds.' The picture provoked hatred of the Communists and placed pressure on the US government to commit more forces to Korea – both objectives desired by General Douglas MacArthur.

correspondent for *Time* after realising that its proprietor Henry Luce would never accept his analysis that Mao Tse-tung and his Communists were destined to supplant the Nationalists. Jack Beldon's 'China Shakes the World' confirmed White's views. Australian Wilfred Burchett, covering the Civil War from the Communist side, added his own incisive analysis, while Carl Mydans kept *Life* magazine supplied with photographs detailing the collapse of Nationalist forces. Despite the warnings, many Americans were shocked by Mao's triumph in 1949, fearing him as a tool of Russian Soviet imperialism.

KOREA

When North Korean forces struck into South Korea on 25 June 1950, America and the West believed that a part of the Cold War had suddenly turned hot. Foremost among them was General Douglas MacArthur, commander of Allied occupation forces in Japan, a right-wing Republican dismayed by the Truman administration's abandonment of Chiang Kai-shek and Nationalist China to Mao Tse-tung's Communists. Knowing that Truman would be reluctant to send troops to Korea, on 27 June MacArthur flew to the front lines, accompanied by a planeload of reporters. MacArthur gave his entourage ideal photo-opportunities. He posed on a hilltop with shells landing in the distance as lines of retreating troops passed by – the hero General standing alone between the free world and the Communist hordes. MacArthur, who had spent two years as press liaison officer in Washington, knew what press

photographers wanted. To firm up America's commitment to a ground war in Korea, MacArthur encouraged *Life* and *Newsweek* to print photos of the bodies of GIs who had been murdered by the North Koreans during their advance. Washington was aghast, cabling 'due to decidedly unfavourable public reaction to recent atrocity pictures and pictures of wounded men in battle areas, strongly recommend no release of this type of picture in battle area'. But MacArthur understood the American public. *Life* and *Newsweek* were inundated with letters complaining that the Truman administration had been caught by surprise, and now had to fight the war properly. As one bereaved father wrote, 'Our sons were not given a fair fighting chance for their lives.'

MacArthur refused to impose censorship on reporters in Korea, trusting their experience and

about 10,000 terrorists in battle, but had another 24,000 Kikuyu concentrated in camps, where there were frequent violent disturbances. In addition, the British rigorously imposed the death penalty for possession of firearms. Some 1,200 Kikuyu went to the scaffold, sometimes several at once. Questions were asked in the British parliament about British counter-insurgency operations in Kenya but the Mau Mau had no real sympathisers in the West.

In Malaya and Kenya the British had been lucky, fighting against easily identifiable minorities like the Chinese squatters or the Kikuyu. In Cyprus they

above

British sweep in the Trudos Mountains, Cyprus, 8 December 1955. Never more than 300 strong, Colonel George Grivas' Eoka terrorists had the support of the vast majority of the Greek population. In four and a half years of fighting against some 30,000 British troops and police, he lost 218 dead and inflicted some 500 dead and wounded on the British. The British had little alternative other than to search villages street by street, a time-consuming process which took years to produce results.

had to protect a Turkish minority, about 20 per cent of the population, from the Greek majority, virtually all of whom wanted 'enosis', union with Greece. Penetration of the Greek Cypriot community proved impossible. In desperation, some British soldiers used excessive violence to interrogate suspects, stories which soon reached the British press. The situation in Cyprus showed that there were limits to the British approach to countering an insurgency, particularly when the insurgency had widespread popular support.

SUEZ

In autumn 1956 the French and British joined forces to strike a killer blow to Arab nationalism, a force undermining their positions in the Middle East. Israel, working in co-operation with Britain and France, attacked into the Sinai on 29 October, which elicited an Anglo–French ultimatum to both Israel and Egypt. When the Egyptians refused the cease-fire, Anglo–French warships and aircraft began bombarding Egyptian air bases and other military installations. It went on for five days, enough time for American opinion to harden and threaten Britain and France with economic collapse if they went ahead. Thinking the Americans were bluffing, Anglo–French forces landed at Port Said on 5 November, and within 48 hours discovered that the United States had pulled the plug on the pound and the franc. Both nations were forced into a humiliating withdrawal, acknowledging at last that they really were living in the American century.

above right

Concentration Camp in Kenya, 1953. In an effort to dry up support for the Mau Mau, the British detained up to 70,000 Kikuyu, including 25,000 rounded up from shanty towns around Nairobi. Some were interrogated and released, some were set free after being 'turned', but a hard core remained in camps until the end of the decade. On 28 July 1959, 11 Mau Mau detainees were killed in a riot in Hola camp, which Labour MPs denounced as a massacre. They called on the Colonial Secretary, Alan Lennox-Boyd, to resign.

'More deadly than the male', Hungary, 1956. Photo-journalists snap a resistance fighter and a dead secret policeman in Budapest, 26 October 1956. For 48 hours, 26–28 October, Hungarian patriots hunted down supporters of the Communist regime, meting out summary justice. The Russians counterattacked on 1 November, bloodily suppressing resistance. Radio Hungary transmitted its last broadcast at 08:10 on 5 November: 'Help Hungary … Help … Help … Help.'

HUNGARY

If the French and British empires were having problems, so too were the Russians. For nearly a decade Voice of America had been beaming promises to the people of Eastern Europe that if they rose up to throw off Soviet chains, America would help them. On 23 October 1953 Hungary did precisely that. Crowds tore down statues of Stalin, and stormed the barracks of the secret police, killing many. On 25 October a pro-western government was formed by Imre Nagy, and western journalists, including Dickey Chapelle, flooded in. Soviet forces – some 200,000 troops and 2,500 tanks – surrounded Budapest and attacked on 1 November. Fighting raged through the city for four days, in which 7,000 Russians and 25,000 Hungarians were killed. The Soviets arrested Dickey Chapelle and held her for three months, but not before she was able to get her best photographs into the West.

right
Seven villagers about to be murdered, My Lai,
16 March 1968. Army photographer Ron Haeberle
spent two hours at My Lai photographing scenes from
hell. His most poignant picture was of a group of women
and children, all terrified and weeping, one of them trying
to do up her shirt, which a soldier was trying to rip off
her. Haeberle's presence gave the group a few extra
seconds of life. When he saw Haeberle with his camera,
one of the Americans called out, 'Whoa! Whoa! Hold it,
guys.' Haeberle took his picture and as he turned away,
'All of a sudden "Bam, bam, bam, bam!" and I looked
around and there's all these people going down.'

ESCALATION

The air campaign was the prelude to massive reinforcement. First in were the Marines, who landed at Da Nang in the north of South Vietnam on 8 March 1965. Journalists who had covered the Second World War and Korea saw Vietnam in much the same terms as the earlier conflicts. David Douglas Duncan, who, though now in his early fifties, covered the war for *Life*, wrote of one battle that the Marines viewed it 'in the same light as Tarawa and Iwo Jima and are proud and happy to have held this hillock in a remote land'. Dickey Chapelle also arrived in Da Nang, and covered five operations with the Marines before she was killed by a land-mine on 18 October 1965, the first American woman photographer to be killed in action. Some of the best action footage was taken by Larry Burrows, a British photographer, who as an 18-year-old laboratory assistant had on 7 June 1944 inadvertently destroyed most of Robert Capa's D-Day pictures. In the spring of 1965 Burrows came close to matching his hero's exploits in a picture essay for *Life*, 'One Ride with Yankee Papa 13', the story of the unsuccessful attempt of a Marine helicopter crew to rescue the crew of a downed helicopter.

Remembering the good relationship that had existed between the military and journalists in Korea, the American army made no attempt to impose censorship in South Vietnam. It would not have been legally possible. Instead, the US military made press accreditation to South Vietnam almost ludicrously easy, and then provided transport and protection once in theatre. Simultaneously picture agencies and magazines were offering substantial premiums for good war photographs. A much younger generation of photo-journalists was soon flooding into Vietnam, people born in the 1930s and 40s who had no direct experience of war, and sometimes very little experience as journalists. Significantly there was also a large number of young women, some of whom had come to Vietnam following boyfriends, and who started freelancing for various agencies. Driven by cut-throat competition for sensational pictures, some of this new generation concentrated on the one per cent of war which is unadulterated horror, removing it from the context of boredom, comradeship and humour – sometimes black – which forms the backdrop of any conflict.

There were several different wars going on in Vietnam simultaneously. Battles in the lightly populated central highlands against regular Viet Cong units, and units of the North Vietnamese Army, became very much like battles on Okinawa or Iwo Jima, where American firepower was brought to bear against heavily entrenched Vietnamese positions. But counter-guerrilla operations in heavily populated areas like the Mekong Delta or the provinces around Saigon invariably produced civilian casualties, and pictures of dead women and children were soon commonplace. These images were not solely responsible for undermining domestic support for the war, but they contributed to the process. Much more significant were announcements in late 1967 that the war was as good as won, and that the next couple of years would be devoted to mopping-up operations.

below
US soldier camped in the Vietnamese jungle,
25 October 1968. Skeletal remains were common
on old battlefields in tropical environments, where flesh
disintegrated very quickly. Such displays of enemy skulls
were not uncommon during the Second World War, from
the Australians in New Guinea, the British in Burma and
the Americans in the Pacific Islands. Yet most officers
and NCOs had stamped hard on the practice, reinforcing
a code of honour which treated all human remains, even
those of a hated enemy, with respect. This picture,
capturing the point at which soldierly pride gives way
to a display of adolescent savagery, shows that by late
1968 the American army was in steep decline.

been wracked by civil war since the American incursion in 1970, but now the country was going to descend into a nightmare as the Khmer Rouge returned the population to the year zero, so that a new and pure society could be built. Thirteen days later the North Vietnamese Army rolled into Saigon, as Vietnamese who had served with or been employed by the Americans fought to break into the compound of the American embassy for a place on the last evacuation helicopters.

America in the mid-1970s was in a state of shock. Defeated in South-East Asia, it also faced threats in the western hemisphere. In 1967 the Bolivian army, with the assistance of American special forces, had run Che Guevara to earth, but in the process had turned him into a revolutionary saint. In 1973 the CIA had snuffed out what looked like a left-wing takeover in Chile, supporting a military coup which toppled President Allende. Unfortunately Allende had been democratically elected and a journalist had been able to take one last photograph showing a bravely determined president wearing a helmet and carrying an automatic rifle, preparing to go down fighting in defence of democratic freedoms. Together Che and Allende inspired a generation of insurgents in Latin and South America, which the United States attempted to fight, sometimes enlisting some unsavoury allies.

above
The last picture of Salvador Allende, outside Chile's presidential palace, 11 September 1973. When the air force bombed the palace after a tense stand-off, Allende ordered his staff to surrender. He then returned to his office, placed the muzzle of an automatic rifle in his mouth and blew his head off. As he hoped, the Junta was blamed for his murder, about the only crime they didn't actually commit.

REVOLUTION IN IRAN

The main challenge continued to come from the Middle East. The linchpin of American power in the Middle East was oil-rich Iran, ruled by a pro-American Shah who had been attempting to westernise and modernise his country. But the programme had gone too quickly for some and not quickly enough for others. His regime faced threats from both Islamic fundamentalists and left-wing radicals, which the

Shah suppressed. In 1979, when the army refused to fire on vast street demonstrations, the Shah and his entourage fled, and was replaced by the violently anti-western theocracy of fundamentalist Ayatollahs. Early the following year revolutionary students stormed the US embassy, and held hostage some 400 embassy personnel. In April the United States launched a clandestine mission to snatch the hostages from under the noses of the revolutionary guards in the heart of Tehran. It ended in bloody failure at a secret landing strip in the Iranian desert, when a C-130 collided with a helicopter. The first the world knew of the operation were pictures from Iran, showing bearded Ayatollahs grinning with satisfaction as they picked through the wreckage. It was another major humiliation for the United States, and spelled the end of Jimmy Carter's presidency.

Early in 1981 America's new president, Ronald Reagan, embarked on a programme of rebuilding the armed forces of the United States, but the miasma of Vietnam seemed to bedevil all efforts. On 6 June 1982, in an effort to be free of continuing cross-border incursions, Israel had struck into Lebanon,

increasingly the home of Palestinian terrorist groups. It had taken Israeli armour only six days to get to Beirut, but a prolonged siege ensued, in which pictures of the Israeli bombardment began to turn world opinion in favour of the Arab cause. An Israeli withdrawal was eventually brokered, with an international peacekeeping force drawn from the USA, France, Italy and Britain entering Beirut. On 23 October 1983 a member of the Iranian-backed Hezbollah (Party of God) drove a truck loaded with 2,000 pounds of explosives directly at US Marine Corps HQ at Beirut airport, killing 241 and seriously injuring 71. The French were hit at exactly the same time, incurring 73 dead and wounded, but it was photographs of the American disaster which flashed around the world.

OPERATION URGENT FURY

Forty-eight hours later US forces landed on the Caribbean island of Grenada, which US intelligence believed was being taken over by revolutionary Marxists, supported by Cubans. The ostensible objective was to rescue US students at an American campus on the island, although commentators believed that the Beirut bomb had accelerated the operation. As this was the first major US operational deployment since Vietnam, the press was tightly controlled. The US deployed overwhelming strength against an enemy which numbered about 500, armed only with light weapons. With the exception of the landing of the Marines on the eastern side of the island, the operation was a fiasco, with special forces losing seven Black Hawk helicopters, while the Rangers and 82nd Airborne were pinned down by a handful of Cuban construction workers. But it took more than three years for the full story to seep out. At the time photographs approved for publication showed 'Urgent Fury' as an outstanding success,

above
United States Marine Corps HQ, Beirut, 23 October 1983. The shock of losing 241 dead to a single blast caused the Americans to lash back at Hezbollah positions in Beirut. Their air attacks and naval bombardment exacerbated the situation. Security had failed to notice that 'Shuffles', the old and lame Arab cleaner, was in fact conducting a reconnaissance for Hezbollah, working out the best time for the truck to attack. From the terrorist perspective the operation was an outstanding success – the first of many suicide bombings.

though the ground commander in Grenada, Major General Norman Schwarzkopf, knew that the US military had not yet recovered from Vietnam.

BRITAIN STRUGGLES BACK

In the early 1980s, when some American generals despaired of ever seeing a US military renaissance, a few took heart from the British experience. In Beirut on 23 October 1983, for example, the British base had been attacked as well, but alert British sentries had shot the truck bomber dead and then deactivated the explosives, events which had been kept very quiet. But Britain's own military reputation had stood at a low ebb at Suez, just 27 years earlier, and it had been a long climb back. In the 1960s and 70s Britain had steadily withdrawn from commitments, sometimes very hastily, as in Aden, and had refused to take any on, even when the moral case was overwhelming, as when former colonies collapsed into chaos. In

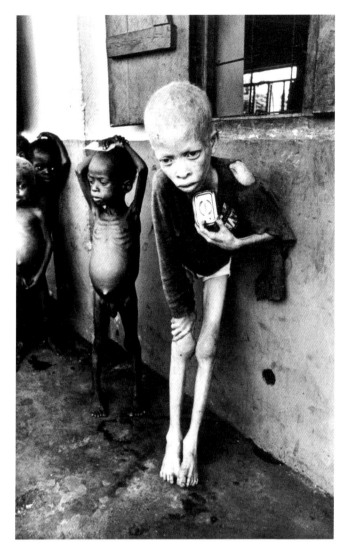

Africa, for example, when Nigeria had fallen into civil war in 1967, the British government ignored a well-orchestrated press campaign to help the stricken breakaway province of Biafra, which the federal government proceeded to starve into submission. Nor did the British do more than offer their good offices to the feuding successors to the Raj, India and Pakistan, who fought short but intense wars in 1965 and 1971.

THE TROUBLES

By the early 1970s Britain seemed to have slipped back into the role of a peripheral and declining European state, beset by its own domestic difficulties. In Northern Ireland the forces of Irish nationalism had re-emerged, with an urban-guerrilla splinter group of the IRA, the Provisional IRA, conducting increasingly effective operations, including a bombing campaign. British troops, who had been sent to the province in 1969 to protect Catholics from Protestants, soon found themselves the target of attack, and responded in a heavy-handed way which made the situation worse. During the long war in Northern Ireland the British army honed its military skills, from small unit actions (section and platoon attacks), force security, special force operations and media management. By the early 1980s, over a quarter of a million troops had passed through Northern Ireland, which was providing excellent training, but which passed relatively unnoticed by the world outside.

right
'Who Dares Wins': a hostage escapes from the burning Iranian embassy, Prince's Gate, 5 May 1980. Britain's Special Air Service, for years little more than a rumour, carried out this spectacular operation in the full glare of publicity. Although it did not go entirely according to plan, it seemed a model of efficiency and daring when compared to other operations, and thrilled the world.

THE FALKLANDS

In 1980, within days of the failure of Operation Eagle's Claw, Britain's shadowy Special Air Service (SAS) came momentarily into the limelight, ending a terrorist siege of the Iranian embassy at London's Prince's Gate in a spectacular but coldly efficient fashion. It was the first time most of the public had ever heard of, let alone seen, the SAS and it sent a ripple of excitement through a public which had had very little to be proud of, at least in a military sense, for nearly a generation. It might have been a passing blip, but for the Argentine invasion of the Falkland Islands on 2 April 1982. Overjoyed with the success of the operation, Argentine cameramen photographed Royal Marine prisoners being forced by gun-waving Argentine special forces to lie on their stomachs on the road outside Government House in Port Stanley. When the photograph was published in Britain, it provoked outrage, ending any real possibility of a negotiated peace. In the ensuing conflict, the press were kept tightly controlled, in part an inevitable response to the lessons of Vietnam, in part the sheer impossibility of it being otherwise, given that they were utterly dependent on the British armed forces 8,000 miles from home. The Falklands was a clean campaign. There were only 2,000 civilians on the islands, and by and large the Argentinians behaved correctly. Only three islanders were killed, when the British accidentally dropped a shell on to Stanley. The land battles were mainly fought at night, and so the photographs tended to be before and after shots of combat, in which the tough professionalism of the British shone through. They were tired, wet, dirty, cold and hungry, but their eyes and faces were not those of demoralised and defeated men. Even the pictures of ships sinking and exploding were taken as indications of British resilience, and an almost-welcome reminder that the war was by no means a walk-over. In Britain the victory was like a collective tonic to an ailing nation. It seemed to indicate that the decline might not be inexorable, that the bottom had been reached and that from now on the country was bouncing back.

AFGHANISTAN

Many Americans were irritated with the British for placing so much store on reclaiming such distant possessions when the Cold War seemed to be entering yet another critical phase. In December 1979, taking advantage of the chaos caused by the Iranian revolution, the USSR invaded Afghanistan, to bolster a reformist Marxist government. The United States and Britain both trained and armed insurgents of the Mujaheddin, ultra-conservative Muslims, and ensured that the USSR would not be able to secure an early peace. Taking advantage of an apparent power vacuum, in September 1980 Saddam Hussein, the secular president of Iraq, had invaded oil-rich Arabistan, the south-westernmost province of Iran. Instead

above
Argentine Commandos (the 'Buzo Tactico') force surrendered Royal Marines to lie on the road outside Government House, Port Stanley, 2 April 1982. When the Argentine commander realised that photographs had been taken, he tried desperately but unsuccessfully to prevent their publication. Appearing in British papers on the morning of Saturday 3 April, the pictures infuriated MPs about to debate the British response to the invasion.

of collapsing, the Iranians fought back effectively, tying Iraq into a war of attrition. The United States,
Britain, and other western nations, now kept Iraq in the field supplying Saddam with modern technology.
The Iraqis used mustard gas to blunt Iranian attacks in the mid-1980s, and also employed gas against
disaffected Kurdish regions in the north, photographs of which were slowly passed to the West. In
addition, the West set up naval patrols in the Gulf, to ensure the free passage of oil tankers. It was a
small sea area and very crowded, and inevitably accidents happened. The Iraqis inadvertently fired an
Exocet at the USS *Stark*, and the USS *Vincennes* shot down an Iranian airliner, believing it to be an
attacking aircraft. In the tragic aftermath, some believe that the Iranians avenged their dead by seeking
the help of Libya's Colonel Gadaffi in placing a bomb on a Pan American flight, which blew up over the
small Scottish town of Lockerbie just before Christmas 1988.

Mired in Afghanistan, the USSR faced yet other pressures. President Reagan's 'Star Wars'
programme, a plan for a space-based anti-ballistic missile system, was designed in part to place
unsupportable economic strain on the USSR, but the danger was that if it succeeded the Soviets might

below
Last Soviet column pulls out of Afghanistan, February 1989. For nearly ten years the USSR had fought a war which bore many similarities to the American campaign in Vietnam. The Soviets held the major cities, but elsewhere their control was weak. Lavishly supplied with American Stinger missiles in the latter part of the campaign, the guerrillas made it too dangerous for the Soviet air force to give close air support to ground forces. Although only about 15,000 Soviet troops died in the conflict, they tended to be special forces or officers, the children of the 'nomenklatura'. Thus the war had a considerable impact on the upper echelons and gave impetus to Gorbachev's reform programme, which proved fatal to the Soviet system. The withdrawal of Soviet forces was treated as a great victory throughout the Islamic world, but the full implications of this success were not immediately apparent to the West.

lash out in a death spasm. There were also signs that Soviet control in Eastern Europe was unravelling, particularly in Poland, where there were strikes and demonstrations. Like Johnson and Nixon when confronted with Vietnam, the new Soviet premier Mikhail Gorbachev adopted a policy of 'Afghanistanisation', and began to withdraw in March 1988. But the attempt to reduce Soviet over-stretch and to liberalise the Soviet regime had come too late. On 15 March 1989 crowds took to the streets in Budapest demanding democracy and national independence, and then it spread like a bush-fire. In Eastern Europe governments generally caved in to popular demands, though in Beijing's Tiananmen Square on 3 June tanks of the People's Army crushed about 2,000 pro-democracy demonstrators. Watched throughout the world, this brutal repression acted like petrol being poured on flames. A non-Communist government was elected in Poland; Latvia, Lithuania and Estonia announced their intention of seeking independence from the USSR; and on 18 October East German president Erich Honecker resigned in the face of mounting disorder. On 9 November the border between East and West Germany was opened for the first time since 1961. The following night crowds in both East and West Berlin, armed with sledge-hammers and pick-axes, began demolishing the wall.

below
Smashing the Iron Curtain, Berlin, 12 November 1989. When the first gap in the wall appeared, East Berliners passed through to the west, to be embraced and kissed by their fellow Germans. As more and more of the wall came down, huge crowds celebrated in what became an enormous street party, with fireworks, music, dancing and large quantities of excellent German lager. In the West there was a moment of self-congratulation; the Cold War had ended in an outright victory. It now seemed possible that the world might indeed enter those 'broad, sun-lit uplands' once envisaged by Winston Churchill at the very darkest period of the twentieth century.

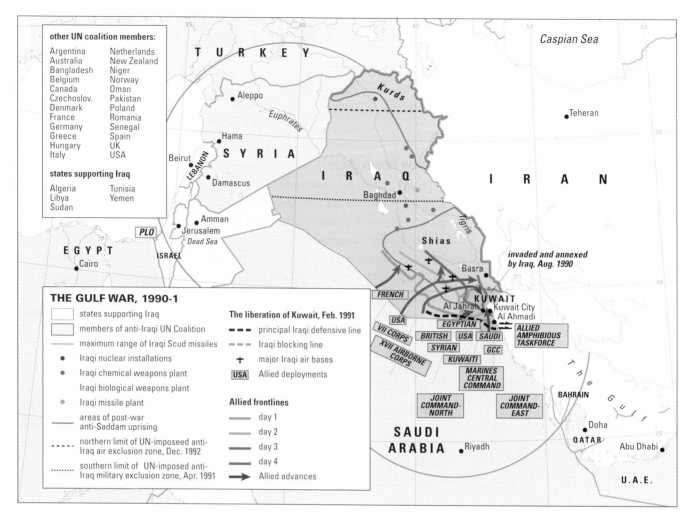

other UN coalition members:

Argentina	Netherlands
Australia	New Zealand
Bangladesh	Niger
Belgium	Norway
Canada	Oman
Czechoslov.	Pakistan
Denmark	Poland
France	Romania
Germany	Senegal
Greece	Spain
Hungary	UK
Italy	USA

states supporting Iraq

Algeria	Tunisia
Libya	Yemen
Sudan	

THE GULF WAR, 1990-1

☐ states supporting Iraq
☐ members of anti-Iraqi UN Coalition
— maximum range of Iraqi Scud missiles
● Iraqi nuclear installations
● Iraqi chemical weapons plant
   Iraqi biological weapons plant
● Iraqi missile plant
— areas of post-war anti-Saddam uprising
- - - northern limit of UN-imposeed anti-Iraq air exclusion zone, Dec. 1992
······ southern limit of UN-imposed anti-Iraq military exclusion zone, Apr. 1991

The liberation of Kuwait, Feb. 1991
- - - principal Iraqi defensive line
- - - Iraqi blocking line
✛ major Iraqi air bases
USA Allied deployments

Allied frontlines
— day 1
— day 2
— day 3
— day 4
➔ Allied advances

invaded and annexed by Iraq, Aug. 1990

It took several weeks for the United States and Britain to stitch together a coalition, and nearly six months for forces and equipment to be shipped to Saudi Arabia. For the first six weeks of the crisis, from 2 August until about 20 September, the Americans lacked forces in place to stop an Iraqi strike south to the ports of Al Jybal and Dhahran. During this period photographs and television footage of the Coalition Commander, General Norman Schwarzkopf, were projected around the world to create the illusion of overwhelming power, in the absence of its actuality. Schwarzkopf might have come from Hollywood Central Casting; known variously as 'Stormin' Norman' or 'The Bear', the growling, six-foot three-inch, 17-stone general looked as though he could have stopped an Iraqi armoured column single-handedly.

The deployment was the largest the Americans had undertaken since Vietnam, and the largest for the British since Suez 44 years earlier. Vietnam had shown them the dangers of free roving journalists, and both forces took steps to control journalist activity. The American media plan Annex Foxtrot, later leaked to the *New York Times*, stated that journalists in the war zone would be 'escorted at all times. Repeat, at all times'. The Americans alone accredited more than 1,400 journalists and there were hundreds more from Britain and France but, with the exception of an independent handful, most were fed information in a media pool at Dhahran. Unsurprisingly the Iraqis did the same, concentrating journalists in a few major hotels in Baghdad, from where they were able to film the beginning of the air campaign on 16 January 1991.

Obsessed with partly learned 'lessons' from Vietnam, the Coalition high command contrived to present the air campaign as 'high-tech' and relatively bloodless. In fact only seven per cent of the ordnance were so-called 'smart' weapons; the remainder used the same technology employed in Vietnam, Korea and

the Second World War. And even 'smart' weapons could kill large numbers of people if they landed in the wrong place. Peter Arnett, a New Zealander working for CNN in Baghdad, earned the Coalition's wrath when he reported from the smouldering ruins of an air-raid shelter in which hundreds of women and children had been sheltering, described in a military briefing as a command and control shelter. When the ground attack began, the Coalition minders discovered that even escorted photo-journalists could capture profoundly disturbing images. One, a picture of the charred but still recognisably human form of an Iraqi tank commander, still in the turret of his tank, was pulled from the AP wire because it was considered too horrific. The London *Observer* published it anyway, provoking a storm of controversy in the liberal media. When photo-journalists and television crews reached the Mutla Ridge, and began filming the carnage that was produced when Coalition air-power had massacred the retreating Iraqis at a choke-point, President Bush decided the time had come to halt military operations, reaffirming the power of an image to influence behaviour.

In March 1991 all the hopes of 1989 seemed to be coming to fruition. For the first time in its history the United Nations had performed in the way its founders had intended, providing the framework for the international community to resist aggression. On 19 August there was a frightening blip, when Communist hardliners in Moscow led by Gennady Yanayev took advantage of reforming premier Mikhail Gorbachev's absence in the Crimea to stage a coup. For 48 hours it seemed that the old order was about to reassert itself, but the hour found its man. On 21 August the world thrilled to the image of Boris Yeltsin, the flamboyant President of the Russian Federation, rallying Muscovites in front of the White House, the Russian Parliament building. The coup collapsed, and then events moved with astonishing rapidity. On 29 August the Russian Parliament suspended the Communist Party, seized its assets and disbanded the KGB. And on 1 January 1992 the Soviet Union ceased to exist. President Bush's determination to create a 'New World Order' at last seemed achievable.

right

Arkan and his Tigers. Described as a 'charming, handsome, psychopathic killer', Arkan, became one of the most notorious warlords in the Balkans. He and his Tigers were directly employed by Serbia's president Slobodan Milosevic to do the dirty work that regular forces had to avoid. On 27 August 1991 the Tigers massacred about 250 patients and staff in the general hospital in the Croatian town of Vukovar. In the spring of 1992 the Tigers stormed and ethnically cleansed the predominantly Muslim towns of Bijeljina and Zvornik in north-east Bosnia, to create a corridor between Serbia proper and the Serbian part of Bosnia.

OR THE NEW WORLD DISORDER?

In the winter of 1991–92 armed forces throughout the West, like the armies of the old Soviet bloc, were being reduced in size. But in the midst of the euphoria there were indications that the celebrations were premature. Far from being the cause of instability it was becoming apparent that the Cold War had subsumed a variety of ethnic, religious and territorial tensions into an over-arching ideological struggle. In many areas of the world long-established patterns of historical evolution had been frozen for more than a generation. With the thaw the evolutionary rivers began flowing once again. The collapse of Communism had not seen the end of history – it had brought history back to life. Nowhere was this more apparent than in the Balkans, where by 1991 the disintegration of Yugoslavia had led to fighting between Serbia and the newly independent republics of Croatia and Slovenia. The former Yugoslavia in the early 1990s allowed journalists the same freedoms but exposed them to even greater dangers than Vietnam in the 1960s or Spain in the 1930s. Would-be Robert Capas and Margaret Bourke Whites, festooned with Nikons, swarmed into the war zone. Some were going to die, many were going to go back to 'proper' jobs, but a few would make it.

THE WARS OF YUGOSLAVIAN DISINTEGRATION, 1991–99

One of the first to reach the Balkans was a 26-year-old New Yorker, Ron Haviv, who had taken up photography as a hobby while a student at New York University. None of those involved in the Balkan bloodletting had a particularly sophisticated awareness of the power of the media, but the Bosnian Serbs were particularly inept. Local warlord Zelijko Raznatovic, known as Arkan, was delighted when Haviv offered to photograph him. Backed by his sinisterly hooded men, holding their AK-47s, Arkan stared menacingly at the camera, holding a sub-machine gun in his right hand and a tiger-cub in his left.

After the first clashes in Slovenia and Croatia, on 25 September 1991 the United Nations imposed a mandatory arms embargo on Yugoslavia, which hurt everyone but the well-

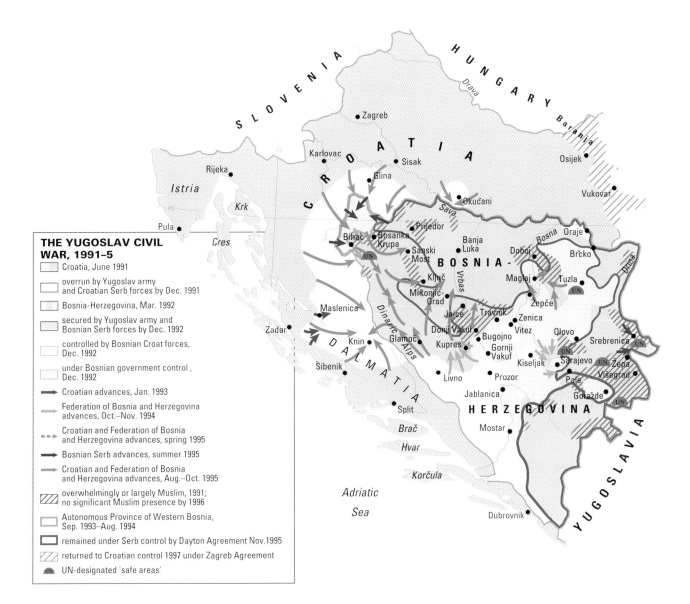

THE YUGOSLAV CIVIL WAR, 1991–5

- Croatia, June 1991
- overrun by Yugoslav army and Croatian Serb forces by Dec. 1991
- Bosnia-Herzegovina, Mar. 1992
- secured by Yugoslav army and Bosnian Serb forces by Dec. 1992
- controlled by Bosnian Croat forces, Dec. 1992
- under Bosnian government control, Dec. 1992
- Croatian advances, Jan. 1993
- Federation of Bosnia and Herzegovina advances, Oct.–Nov. 1994
- Croatian and Federation of Bosnia and Herzegovina advances, spring 1995
- Bosnian Serb advances, summer 1995
- Croatian and Federation of Bosnia and Herzegovina advances, Aug.–Oct. 1995
- overwhelmingly or largely Muslim, 1991; no significant Muslim presence by 1996
- Autonomous Province of Western Bosnia, Sep. 1993–Aug. 1994
- remained under Serb control by Dayton Agreement Nov.1995
- returned to Croatian control 1997 under Zagreb Agreement
- UN-designated 'safe areas'

above

The Yugoslav Civil War, 1991–95. Bosnia was the epicentre of the conflict. Its three million people – Roman Catholic Croats, Eastern Orthodox Serbs and Bosnian Muslims – lived jumbled together in an ethnic and cultural patchwork quilt. Older historical conflicts fuelled the war. Fifty years earlier Croats of the Fascist Ustashi, Muslims of the SS Handschar Division, and Serbs of Tito's and Mihailovich's partisan units, fought a bitter war in Bosnia, rekindling ancient hatreds which exploded into life in the post-Communist 1990s. A conflict between warrior bands, without clear front lines, it recalled the seventeenth-century Scottish highlands, or Germany during the Thirty Years War.

below, opposite

A terrified Muslim on his way to interrogation, Bijeljina, April 1992. Ron Haviv recalled that the young man 'looked me straight in the eyes, pleading for help, but there was absolutely nothing I could do except photograph him'. He was one of the more than 100,000 who perished. Published in *Time* in March 1993, Haviv's photographs did much to condemn the Serbs in the world's eyes. Yet Croat and Muslim militias proved just as brutal.

equipped Serbs, who had inherited most of the old federal army. By the spring of 1992 civil war had broken out in Bosnia, with Bosnian Serbs supported by federal forces blockading and shelling Sarajevo, Bosnia's capital. In predominantly Serb areas tens of thousands of Muslims and Croats were on the move, their lives threatened and their homes burnt. Where they resisted they were massacred. No one knows exactly how many died in 1992, the worst year in the Balkans, but the United Nations estimated that it was at least 130,000. Young men of military age who were not killed were herded into concentration camps, where they were left to die of starvation. That summer Ron Haviv discovered one such camp at Trnopolje and his pictures appalled the world.

The pictures pouring in from the Balkans provoked action, but it proved inadequate. The United Nations' new protection force (UNPROFOR), tasked with providing humanitarian relief, amounted to only 23,000. Bosnian Muslims and Croats soon came to see UNPROFOR as another enemy. The United Nations declared certain towns 'safe areas' under UN protection, but then failed to protect them. UN humiliation seemed inevitable. On 11 July 1995 a Bosnian Serb army overran Srebrenica, one of the larger safe areas. Oblivious to the presence of the world's press, they systematically killed 8,000 unarmed male Muslims, ranging from boys to old men.

The destruction of Srebrenica effectively ended the United Nations mission, but the United States had already embarked on a different policy. On 11 November 1994 it had abandoned the arms embargo in order to arm Muslims and Croats, believing a balance of military capability might restore peace. In early August 1995 a re-equipped and well-trained Croatian army, supported by NATO (American) air power, launched Operation Storm. This succeeded in breaking Serbian resistance in the Krajina, and sent a flood

THE CRISIS IN KOSOVO, 1999

flight of Kosovan Albanian refugees, Mar.–May 1999

towns bombed by NATO forces, Mar.-June 1999

sites of religious significance to Serbs

NATO zone of occupation with nationality of occupying force

KLA strongholds

major massacres

left

The Crisis in Kosovo, 1999. Serbia's southernmost province was the ancestral home of the Serb people, site of the 1389 Battle of Kosovo. In the three-month air campaign NATO's 10,484 air-strikes were able to hit big stationary targets, but did little damage to Serbian forces, who decoyed hundreds of expensive 'smart' weapons on to microwave ovens. It was the withdrawal of any prospect of Russian support, rather than the air campaign, or even the prospect of a ground assault that broke Belgrade's resistance.

of 250,000 Serbs fleeing east towards Belgrade. On 30 August another heavy air bombardment on Serb positions around Sarajevo finally forced them to accept an agreement negotiated and signed in Dayton, Ohio on 25 November 1995. Bosnia was now to become a military protectorate of the international community. The situation could not last, but at least the killing had stopped.

Less than six months later, fighting flared up in Kosovo, Serbia's southernmost province, the now predominantly Albanian core of the former medieval Serbian state. The Kosovo Liberation Army (KLA) initially comprised a few gangs, but in 1997 as Albania itself slipped into disintegration, arms and trained men flooded across the border. By 1998 the KLA's demands for Kosovan independence increased the danger of a general conflagration in the southern Balkans also involving Macedonia, Bulgaria, Greece and possibly Turkey. On 24 March 1999 after Serbia refused to admit NATO forces, NATO launched an extensive bombing campaign, which hardened rather than weakened Serbian resolve. Serbian forces drove tens of thousands of Kosovar Albanians across the frontier into Macedonia.

left
Albanian refugees pour across the Kosovo–Macedonian frontier, March 1999. The photograph could have been taken by Herbert Baldwin nearly 90 years earlier, so little seemed to have changed. But these refugees were the unintended consequence of high-technology NATO air-strikes on Serbia, which Serb forces sought to counter by pushing hundreds of thousands of Albanians into Macedonia, thereby imposing a massive humanitarian crisis on fragile NATO logistics. Arkan's Tigers, highly experienced in ethnic cleansing in Bosnia, worked alongside regular Serbian forces.

The bombing went on until the second week in June. NATO lacked sufficient ground forces to invade. Serb resolve was weakened when Boris Yeltsin, accepting an American offer of 30 billion dollars in credits to Russia, withdrew traditional Russian military support for Serbia. The NATO commander in Macedonia, General Mike Jackson, managed to negotiate a peaceful withdrawal of the Serbian army, but at the last minute a small Russian column from Bosnia raced down to Pristina, the predominantly Serb capital of Kosovo, where they were treated as heroes. Ordered by NATO commander General Wesley Clark to helicopter forces to Pristina to face down the Russians, Jackson refused, saying, 'General, I'm not going to start World War III for you.'

HEART OF DARKNESS

During the 1990s many areas of the world slipped into chaos. In Africa the mood was at first optimistic. South Africa avoided the long-predicted blood-bath, experiencing a relatively peaceful transition from white minority to black majority rule. In December 1992 the United States landed Marines at Mogadishu

right
Dead American Ranger dragged through the streets of Mogadishu, 3 October 1993. This image reached the West as video footage and as a series of stills snapped by Paul Watson of the *Toronto Star*. The Somalis also turned on Watson, but he was saved by the cameras which hung around his neck. They understood that his cameras were the only way the world would learn of their victory over the Americans. The power of the still photograph to act as a catalyst in certain situations was confirmed when President Clinton ordered the withdrawal of US forces.

opposite
Bosnian Serb commander General Ratko Mladic and the commander of the Dutch UN company, Lieutenant Colonel Thom Karremans, toast the agreement which will hand Srebrenica over to the Serbs, Srebrenica, 11 July 1995. In March 1993 UN commander General Philippe Morillon had promised the Bosnians of Srebrenica, 'We will never abandon you.' A month later the town had been declared a UN protected area. Yet Karremans' nerve cracked when he found himself surrounded by Serb forces, including Arkan's Tigers, and UN high command refused his requests for air strikes. The Dutch secured the evacuation of 23,000 women and children to Muslim areas, but stood by as the Serbs marched off all males aged between 12 and 77 for 'interrogation for suspected war crimes'. When a report into the massacres was finally published in 2002 the Dutch government resigned. Many of the Dutch soldiers suffered severe psychological problems, some claiming they would have preferred to have died fighting than to be forced to live with the shame.

in Somalia, their mission to feed the population. There was a moment of high farce when they came ashore ready for combat, and were dazzled by the flash-bulbs of a mob of photographers and television teams waiting for them, but Christmas 1992 saw President George Bush mobbed by cheering crowds as he made a triumphal procession through Mogadishu. The incoming Clinton administration expanded the mission from humanitarian relief to the rebuilding of the Somali nation, a noble but horrendously difficult task. In an attempt to eliminate one source of instability, on 3 October 1993 400 US Rangers descended by helicopter into central Mogadishu on a cordon-and-search operation to arrest Mohammed Aidid, the most powerful of the Somali warlords. The warlike Somalis gave the Rangers a hot reception; in seven hours of fighting they shot down two Black Hawk helicopters and inflicted 95 casualties on the Rangers, 18 of whom were killed. A photographer from the *Toronto Star* took pictures of Somali mobs dragging the mutilated bodies of naked Rangers through the streets, images which induced the Clinton administration to abandon the mission.

After Somalia the mood in Washington changed – henceforth the US gave up any pretence to global policing. On 12 April 1994, six days after the Hutus of Rwanda turned on their Tutsi neighbours in a frenzy of bloodletting, American reporter Donatella Lorche entered Kigali in a Red Cross medical convoy from Burundi. She reported that the roads were clogged with fleeing refugees. 'Bodies lay everywhere. Several

right

Bodies of murdered Tutsis, Rwanda, April 1994 President Habyarimana had established amongst the majority Hutu population a militia, the Interahamwe, which received its orders via Radio Libre des Milles Collines. About 800,000 Tutsi and moderate Hutu were murdered in 100 days of blood-letting, which ended only when the largely Tutsi Rwandan Patriotic Front overran the country, sending two million Hutu fleeing for their lives into the eastern Congo.

truckloads of frenzied screaming men waving machetes and screwdrivers drove by. At night, screams followed by automatic gunfire could be heard from the churches in Kigali.' Yet these horrific pictures failed to move the US administration. European countries were no keener to get involved. Western media coverage of Hutus fleeing from vengeful Tutsis led to a belated humanitarian effort, with France sending forces to protect refugees from a danger already past. The response to the Rwanda massacres established a pattern for western involvement in Africa. They would intervene to resolve relatively small problems (the British in Sierra Leone in 1999, France in the Ivory Coast in 2002 and the United States in Liberia in 2003) but were reluctant to tackle the vast and unpredictable.

The mid- and late 1990s saw a mood of neo-isolationism sweeping over the United States. The world's only remaining superpower proved reluctant to shoulder the burdens its status demanded. It remained happy to continue operating as a regional power, policing the western hemisphere in ways which Theodore Roosevelt and Woodrow Wilson would have understood. On 20 December 1989, 27,000 US troops had swept into Panama, forcing General Noriega, Panama's self-appointed 'Maximum Leader', to seek refuge in the Papal Nunciatura, the sovereign territory of the Vatican. Here he was forced to surrender on 3 January 1990 by the Americans playing heavy metal rock music through loudspeakers, non-stop. On 19 September 1994 American forces landed in Haiti to restore order. And throughout this period America gave covert support to counter-insurgency campaigns in Central and South America. Occasionally a stunning success was achieved – the arrest and incarceration of Guzman, leader of Peru's Shining Path Guerrillas. But it was mainly an unglamorous and low-key war fought in the shadows, typified by the struggle with Columbian cocaine barons.

Russia, too, concentrated on problems close to home. On 4 October 1993 world TV cameras and photo-journalists assembled outside the Russian Parliament building in Moscow. They captured the assault by pro-Yeltsin forces to end a rebellion by the followers of Vice Presdient Rutskoi. Russia was very far from being a stable liberal-democracy. Nor was the Russian Federation particularly stable. On 11 December 1994 Russian armoured columns invaded the breakaway republic of Chechenya in the Caucasus, and were smashed to pieces in a Chechen ambush in the streets of Grozny. A major urban battle developed, and Grozny, a large city of high-rise reinforced-concrete buildings, soon resembled Stalingrad. Western newsmen, infiltrating the city through Chechen lines, kept the papers of New York and London filled with images of burning Russian armour amidst mountains of rubble. Chechen terrorists carried the war into Russia, bombing government buildings, barracks and hospitals. In the spring of 2003 they seized the Moscow State Theatre, prompting a bloodily inept rescue operation being carried out by the police and army.

above

Abimael Guzman, leader of Peru's Sendero Luminoso guerrillas, goes on trial, Lima, September 1992. A former professor of political philosophy at Lima University, Guzman founded the Maoist guerrilla organisation in 1980. Its liberation philosophy appealed to Lima sophisti-cates. However, it also appealed to illiterate Andean peasants, many of whom could only speak Quechua, the ancient language of the Incas, where Shining Path invoked memories of the Inca empire, and the worship of the sun god. At their height in the early 90s Guzman's guerrillas controlled about 30 per cent of Peru, and had a hard core of at least 10,000 fighters.

With the exception of Africa and the fringes of the Russian federation, as the twentieth century came to an end the mood of optimistic self-congratulation which had characterised 1989 began to return. Many problems seemed on the wane: there was a real prospect of peace in Northern Ireland; the Balkans appeared quiet; and in Cambodia in 1993 and East Timor in 1999, UN interventions, underwritten by the power of the United States, had brought a degree of stability to two of Asia's trouble-spots.

CLASH OF CULTURES

Yet peace was far from imminent in the Muslim world, the vast swathe of territory running from Morocco on the Atlantic to the Philippines in the Pacific. In 1998 Harvard Professor Samuel Huntington had argued that whereas conflict in the twentieth century had been driven by competing ideologies, in the twenty-first century it would involve a clash of cultures and civilisations between the West and Islam. His analysis provoked a storm of criticism – the 'West' came in many forms, as did Islam – but there was much evidence to support it. In 1979 Islamic theocracy triumphed in Iran, a reaction to a process of enforced westernisation; and in 1989 the Soviets, bent on modernising and secularising, had been driven from Afghanistan. In December 1991 the people of Algeria elected a radical Islamic government, only to have the army conduct a coup and establish a military dictatorship with the tacit consent of the West. Everywhere Islam saw itself beleaguered, whether in Bosnia, in the disputed province of Kashmir or in the southern Philippines. Israel's occupation since 1967 of the territories on the West Bank of the Jordan River had in the 1980s created the *Intifada* (the shaking off), with its crowds of stone-flinging children. Under intense American pressure Israel conceded a limited degree of autonomy to a Palestinian entity:

but this created enclaves from where terrorist bombers and suicide bombers could easily operate.

Throughout the decade there had been worrying indications that extremist Islamic groups would hit targets well beyond Israel. On 26 February 1993 a large bomb was detonated in the parking lot under the 110-storey New York World Trade Centre, a symbol of western economic dominance. British journalists, used to covering IRA outrages, were convinced that the terrorists had intended to bring the entire structure crashing down. This time New Yorkers were lucky; only six of the 50,000 people were killed, though about 1,000 were injured. The bombers were quickly traced and arrested. All from the Middle East, they were small fry, acting under the direction of Ramzi Ahmed Yousef, a lieutenant of Osama bin Laden, a wealthy Saudi Arabian who in the 1980s had been one of the principal recruiters and fundraisers for the fundamentalist Mujaheddin. Following the Soviet withdrawal from Afghanistan he had formed an organisation called al-Qaeda (the base), ostensibly to provide support for redundant guerrillas, including the funding of a massive multi-volume official history of the war in Afghanistan, which included helpful hints on guerrilla operations, and which became a best-seller in Pakistan and Iran. Proud of their defeat of the Soviets (the first Muslim victory over Europeans since the Turks drove the Greeks into the sea at Smyrna in 1923), al-Qaeda decided to wage war against the United States, and the regimes it supported.

Operating first from the Sudan and then from Afghanistan, bin Laden orchestrated a world-wide terror campaign. Attempts to assassinate Crown Prince Abdullah of Jordan in June 1993 and President Mubarak of Egypt in June 1995 were followed on 25 June 1996 by a truck bomb at the Al Khobar Towers in Saudi Arabia, which killed 19 and wounded 385 US service personnel. On 7 August 1998 al-Qaeda blew up US embassies in Dar es Salaam and Nairobi, killing more than 200 and injuring about 4,000, which provoked

above
Police survey the damaged underground car-park of the World Trade Centre, New York, 23 February 1993. The operation was ludicrously easy. A group of four Middle Eastern terrorists hired a van, packed it with explosives and parked it under the World Trade Centre, without once arousing suspicion, let alone being challenged. It was only when one of the conspirators tried to get his deposit back from the rental company from which he had hired the van that police got the lead they needed. The failure of the explosion to bring down the building led engineers to conclude that the building was structurally sound; this led to a complacency which proved tragic.

left
Osama bin Laden addresses a news conference in Afghanistan, 26 May 1998. Snapped on one of the last occasions when he appeared in public, this picture has come to assume an iconic status, both for those who draw inspiration from him, and those who wish to see him dead. Bin Laden's love of tradition (his beard and dress) did not extend to his wrist-watch, an expensive Swiss model. Like bin Laden, key members of al-Qaeda combine the certainties of a medieval world view with the willing-ness to exploit all that modern technology can offer.

far left
Suicide bombing on commuter bus, Jerusalem, 11 June 2003. Rescue workers remove the 16 dead and more than 100 injured from what is now an all too common sight in the streets of Israel's cities. The worst suicide bombing of a bus thus far took place in February 1996, when 26 people were killed and 80 injured. In 2002 there were two bus bombings, one which killed 19 and wounded 50, and the other which killed 11 and injured 40. Commuter buses packed with school children and office workers are the sui-cide bomber's preferred target. They are difficult to protect and guarantee a large number of murdered and maimed.

the US into an ineffectual cruise-missile attack on suspected al-Qaeda bases in Afghanistan on 20 August 1998. By the late 1990s intelligence services throughout western countries with Islamic populations were reporting an unusually large movement of young Muslim men to Pakistan and possibly Afghanistan. Britain's MI5 estimated that as many as 2,000 British Muslims had left to spend time in training camps in Afghanistan in 1998 alone. Events like the suicide bombing of the USS *Cole* in Aden harbour on 12 October 2000 served to stimulate recruitment further.

9/11

Yet the United States remained in a fool's paradise, its intelligence agencies misinterpreting the growing wealth of information pointing to something imminent and spectacular. James Nachtwey, a contract photographer for *Time* magazine, arrived back in New York from an assignment in Europe on 10 September 2001. He had a good view of the World Trade Centre from his apartment and heard the first explosion

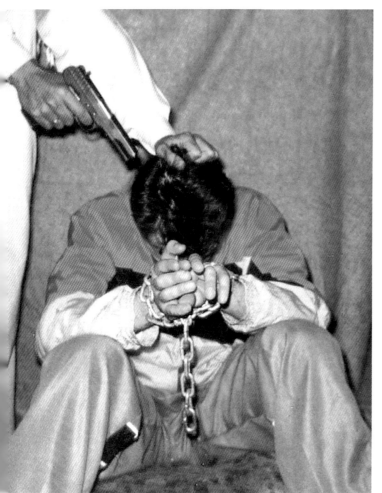

quite clearly. Grabbing his camera, he headed into an area from which everyone else was fleeing. He recalled: 'I was two blocks from the first tower when it collapsed and I photographed the cloud of debris as it boiled through the canyons of lower Manhattan. I made my way through the smoke to photograph the skyscraper where it lay in ruins in the street … Then I heard what sounded like a huge waterfall in the sky. I looked up and saw the second tower falling straight down at me.' Nachtwey realised there wasn't time to take a picture – he ran, and he survived. War correspondent Bill Biggart was also taking pictures and couldn't resist the shot of a lifetime. His camera, miraculously undamaged, was found lying near his body a day later, the final frame an image of the second tower as it began to implode.

THE WAR AGAINST TERROR

The attack on the World Trade Centre, and the simultaneous attack on the Pentagon, cost 3,000 lives, more than were lost at Pearl Harbor. Like that event, Nine Eleven (as it soon became known) roused the American population to a righteous anger, but it also dangerously polarised the world. What came to be called the Anglosphere – at its core the United States, Britain and Australia – closed ranks. In October 2001 American special forces, supported particularly by troops from Britain and Australia, arrived in Afghanistan to co-ordinate the employment of massive American airstrikes in support of the Northern Alliance, a coalition of clans and tribes who had been waging war against the Taliban for nearly ten years. Kabul was taken with surprising ease, but the core of al-Qaeda had already fled. Western journalists combed Pakistan, hoping for a lead to Osama bin Laden, and some got too lucky. On 23 January 2002 *Wall Street Journal* correspondent Daniel Pearl was kidnapped by Islamic militants, who killed him eight days later.

During the spring several other soft targets were hit around the world, particularly western tourists in Islamic countries. By the summer of 2002 a number of nations who had initially supported the American-led campaign began to distance themselves from further operations, leaving the Anglosphere looking isolated, though when asked whether this worried him the Australian Prime Minister John Howard replied, 'No – it was the same in 1942.' The drawing together of the Anglosphere was confirmed by a car bomb outside a Bali nightclub in October 2002, which killed more than 200 and maimed hundreds more, the great majority British and Australians, many of them young women.

The attacks of 9/11, and the subsequent outrages, brought into sharp relief the likelihood – indeed, the certainty – that terrorist groups would soon acquire nuclear weapons, and biological and chemical weapons only slightly less terrifying in their effect. Since the early 1990s desperate efforts (not entirely successful) had been made to monitor the disposal of the vast nuclear arsenal of the Soviet Union, but there was also the danger posed by so-called rogue states, who might fund the private development of weapons of mass destruction, or might launch their own programme of development. Foremost amongst these states was Iraq. In tandem with an information campaign designed to prepare public opinion, from September 2002 to March 2003 some 250,000 US personnel, joined by 47,000 British and 2,000 Australians, deployed to Kuwait. On 20 March, supported by massive air attacks, the British struck towards Basra, the Americans attacked directly into central Iraq, while American special forces, accompanied by the Australians, cut Iraq's communications with Syria to the West. American forces

above
Paddy's Bar, Bali, 12 October 2002. The bombs killed 202 and maimed hundreds more. Indonesian investigators identified the organisation responsible as Jemaah Islamiah, a radical Moslem group who had already carried out numerous attacks on the country's Christian minority. Australia lost the largest number. Despite a warning from bin Laden that 'the Australian crusaders' would be punished for the East Timor intervention, Bali was a bitter disappointment to Australian neo-isolationists who had hoped they could escape involvement in the war on terror.

opposite
American soldiers prepare to pull down a giant statue of Saddam Hussein, Baghdad, 9 April 2003. In a famous address before the attack, Lieutenant Colonel Tim Collins, commanding officer of Britain's Royal Irish Regiment, told his men 'We go to liberate, not to conquer. We will not fly our flags in their country.' In the excitement of the moment, however, Corporal Edward Chin draped the Stars and Stripes over Saddam's face. This widely published still has been used throughout the Muslim world to suggest that America was bent on conquest.

Iraq, 2003. Unlike 1991, Iraq's neighbours in 2002, particularly Saudi Arabia, were reluctant to play host to large American or British forces. An attack, then, would have to come through Turkey but at the last minute the Turkish parliament refused permission. The first two months of 2003 saw a hurried redeployment, with virtually all forces re-routed to Kuwait. On paper Saddam's forces still looked formidable, but the men were badly trained and the equipment a generation out of date. The Coalition was an élite strike force. It took less than three weeks to occupy the country. Unfortunately the infrastructure of the Iraqi state collapsed along with its army.

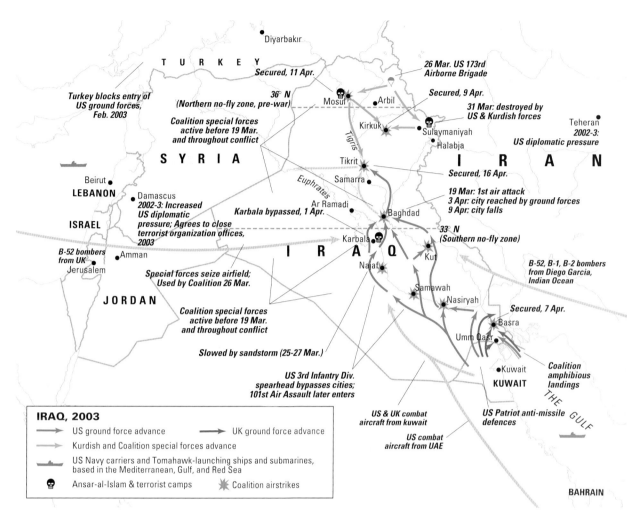

IRAQ, 2003

→ US ground force advance → UK ground force advance

→ Kurdish and Coalition special forces advance

⚓ US Navy carriers and Tomahawk-launching ships and submarines, based in the Mediterranean, Gulf, and Red Sea

☠ Ansar-al-Islam & terrorist camps ✳ Coalition airstrikes

Labels on map:
- Diyarbakır
- TURKEY
- Secured, 11 Apr.
- 26 Mar. US 173rd Airborne Brigade
- Turkey blocks entry of US ground forces, Feb. 2003
- 36°N (Northern no-fly zone, pre-war)
- Mosul
- Arbil
- Secured, 9 Apr.
- 31 Mar: destroyed by US & Kurdish forces
- Teheran 2002-3: US diplomatic pressure
- Coalition special forces active before 19 Mar. and throughout conflict
- Kirkuk
- Sulaymaniyah
- Halabja
- SYRIA
- Tigris
- IRAN
- Beirut
- Tikrit
- LEBANON
- Damascus
- Euphrates
- Samarra
- Secured, 16 Apr.
- 2002-3: Increased US diplomatic pressure; Agrees to close terrorist organization offices, 2003
- Karbala bypassed, 1 Apr.
- Ar Ramadi
- Baghdad
- 19 Mar: 1st air attack
- 3 Apr: city reached by ground forces
- 9 Apr: city falls
- ISRAEL
- Karbala
- 33°N (Southern no-fly zone)
- B-52 bombers from UK
- Amman
- Jerusalem
- IRAQ
- Najaf
- Kut
- B-52, B-1, B-2 bombers from Diego Garcia, Indian Ocean
- Special forces seize airfield; Used by Coalition 26 Mar.
- JORDAN
- Samawah
- Nasiryah
- Secured, 7 Apr.
- Coalition special forces active before 19 Mar. and throughout conflict
- Basra
- Slowed by sandstorm (25-27 Mar.)
- Umm Qasr
- Coalition amphibious landings
- US 3rd Infantry Div. spearhead bypasses cities; 101st Air Assault later enters
- US & UK combat aircraft from kuwait
- US Patriot anti-missile defences
- THE GULF
- Kuwait
- KUWAIT
- US combat aircraft from UAE
- BAHRAIN

were differently structured from those which had fought under Schwarzkopf. They were much lighter and much more dependent on air support, and on a few occasions they were held up by surprisingly determined resistance, but by 9 April US Marines were in Iraq and cheering Shiites were tearing down statues of Saddam Hussein. On 14 April American forces entered Tikrit, Saddam's home town, and centre of his power, and on 1 May President Bush declared major combat operations at an end.

It was premature. Iraqi divisions had collapsed too quickly, and a power vacuum had been created. As the situation slipped into guerrilla war, observers began making comparisons with Vietnam, but they were wrong. They were in a situation which William Howard Russell, Felice Beato and John Burke would have understood only too well. As Russell had once said of the British, the Americans and their friends were now 'empiring it around the world'. No one in Washington had planned this, just as no one in London had quite planned the expansion of the British Empire.

At the dawn of the new century opportunities for the war photographers – those who wish to understand and record the complexities of combat – and photographers of war – those who dwell on the consequences – were never greater.

Index

Picture credits

Associated Press, AP 92t; 125; 129; 133; 139t; 157; 160; 162; 163; 165b; 167b; 173; 180b; 184r; 185b; 185t; 187. **Bettmann/CORBIS** 25; 29; 60; 61; 69; 71; 76; 78; 80b; 88b; 99; 104r; 107b; 107t; 134t; 141; 143; 144; 155; 166t. **Contact Press/Don McCullin** 169b; 169t. **CORBIS** 2; 31; 46; 59; 72t; 98r; 120; 128r; 132b; 136l; 137b; 139b; 145; 146l; 147; 165t; 168r; 176; 182t. **CORBIS SABA** 184t (Ricki Rosen). **CORBIS SYGMA** 167t; 168l (PIERCE BILL); 181 (Watson). **The Edgar Snow Collection** 109; 110; 111. **Gamma** 170b. **Getty Images** 171t; 184b. **Hulton Archive** 9; 11b; 11t; 12; 15b; 15t; 16; 17; 18; 20; 21; 22; 23; 24; 27; 32; 33; 34b; 34t; 35; 36; 39; 40; 41b; 41t; 42; 43; 45b; 48; 49; 50; 51; 52; 63; 64b; 64t; 65t; 66; 67; 68; 70; 72bl; 74; 80t; 81; 83; 84; 86; 91; 92c; 94; 95; 96l; 98l; 100; 101; 104l; 115b; 126t; 137t; 150b; 152r; 154; 161; 164r; 166b. **Hulton-Deutsch Collection/CORBIS** 5; 53; 55; 73; 87; 88t; 89; 93; 105; 106; 112; 113b; 113t; 123; 126b; 146r; 152l; 153; 158; 170t. **Imperial War Museum** 92b. **Kansas State Historical Society** 45t. **Larry Towell / Magnum Photos** 183. **Minnesota Historical Society/CORBIS** 47. **The Museum at Sonderborg Castle, Denmark** 37. **National Army Museum** 13, 56, 57. **National Library of Australia** 96r. **Popperfoto.com** 115t; 132t; 136b; 150t; 151. **Reuters News Media Inc.** 171b; 177; 180t; 182b; 186. **Rex** 175. **Robert Capa R / Magnum Photos** 116; 117; 119; 121; 128l; 136tr; 149. **Ron Haviv/VII** 178b; 178t. **Stuart Franklin / Magnum Photos** 172. **Time Life Pictures/Getty Images** 130 (MARGARET BOURKE WHITE); 134b (GEORGE STROCK); 6 (LARRY BURROWS); 159 (RONALD HAEBERLE); 164l (CECIL J. POSS). **TRH Pictures** 135. **Underwood & Underwood/CORBIS** 85; 103.

t=top
b=bottom
r=right
l=left
c=centre